A Beginners' Guide to
RUBBER
STAMPING

A Beginners' Guide to
RUBBER STAMPING

Brenda Hunt

Guild of Master Craftsman Publications Ltd

First published 1998 by
Guild of Master Craftsman Publications Ltd,
166 High Street, Lewes,
East Sussex BN7 1XU

ISBN 1 86108 092 1

Photography by Gavin Mist
Line drawings by Richard Hawke
Cover photography by Zul Mukhida

Acknowledgements

The publishers and the author would like to thank the following British,
American and Canadian manufacturers and suppliers of rubber stamps
for their permission to use copyright designs in this book: Magenta,
Superstamp, Inca Stamp, Funstamps, Stamps Unlimited,
Rubber Stampede, Personal Impression, Mostly Animals,
First Class Stamps, and All Night Media.

The spiral sun motif used inside and on the cover of this book
was adapted from Primitive Sun (© Rubber Stampede 6104)
and Swirl (© Rubber Stampede 61007)

Readers should take note that copyright rubber stamp designs
are for personal, non-commercial use only.

Cover illustration features the following stamps
Maple Leaf (© Rubber Stampede no 272 D)
Swallowtail (© Inca Stamp no 415 D)
A Bee (© Inca Stamp no 432 D)

Designed by Teresa Dearlove
Typefaces: Friz Quadrata and Berkeley
Colour origination by Viscan Graphics (Singapore)
Printed and bound by Kyodo Printing (Singapore) under the
supervision of MRM Graphics, Winslow, Buckinghamshire, UK

CONTENTS

Dedication

To my niece, Jennifer, for her
invaluable help as a hand model.

INTRODUCTION

Rubber stamping is a hobby that has been steadily growing in popularity and availability, but although it is a relatively new craft form, it has roots which reach far back into printing history. Printing with a design on a block has been done over the centuries with the humble potato cut, lino cutting, the old wood-cutting techniques and copper plate engravings, and when you realise this, you can see just how versatile a printing method rubber stamping can be.

You can decorate almost anything with a selection of rubber stamps and the right choice of ink or paint. Fabrics, ceramics, wood, walls, glass, furniture and wall tiles can all be transformed.

As this book is intended to introduce you to the techniques and styles of rubber stamping, I have concentrated on the various methods and materials that can be used on paper and card projects.

Each new project will help you to develop the skills you have already covered and to add a new technique, material or method of using your rubber stamp art.

I have used a wide variety of designs from different rubber stamp companies and this will give you some idea of what is available. There is a huge range of rubber stamp designs for you to choose from when you start building your own collection. There are updated catalogues available all the time, offering new ink and pigment colours, more embossing powders, new tools to expand your range and, of course, more rubber stamp designs to inspire you to create more rubber stamp art.

Together, the projects form a complete course, taking you from simple techniques at the beginning through to more complex tasks, but I have also tried to design each project to stand alone, so that you can dip into the book as you require a gift box, a birthday card or a photo frame. As you expand your skills, you will see that even the most basic printing methods can still be used to great effect. There are many items that I still print just using a single rubber stamp and an ink pad.

Ultimately I hope the book will inspire you to create new and individual pieces of rubber stamp art as you explore the ever expanding possibilities of this most versatile of printing techniques.

MATERIALS AND EQUIPMENT

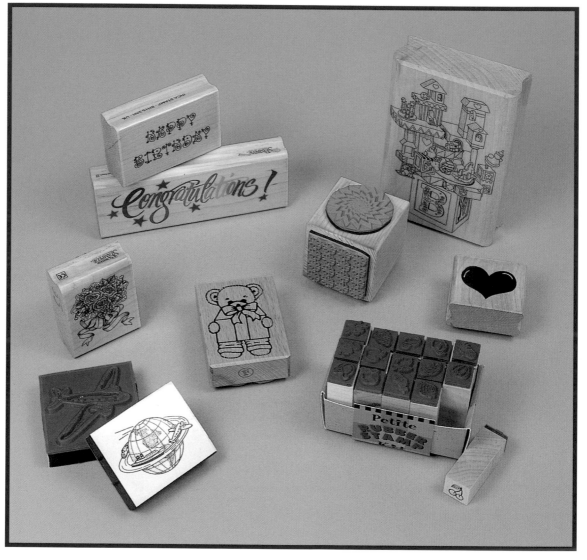

The craft of rubber stamping has been gaining in popularity over the past few years, and many people have been tempted by cute images calling to them from craft shop displays. But once you have decorated a few sheets of notepaper or half a dozen Christmas cards, where do you go from there with your rubber stamp art?

Well, far from hiding them at the back of a cupboard, the scope for these wonderful little design blocks is almost endless, as I hope to show you in this book.

The very name 'rubber stamp' can be misleading, although of course they are rubber and they are made to stamp an image. Too often the phrase 'rubber stamp' brings to mind those name and address stamps that were once used in business, with which it was almost impossible to get a legible impression on any paperwork and the end result consisted mainly of blisters on your hand. Nothing could be further from that than the new world of rubber stamping. It can be a hobby that takes over your life, as well as a lot of space in your home!

The range of rubber stamps is enormous, from beautiful botanical drawings to cute cartoons, tribal designs to elegantly scripted phrases, teddy bears and clowns to dragons and castles. Whatever your taste, there is something out there to interest you, and once you've chosen a design the choices don't end there. The ink that you use, whether you emboss the design, or colour the image, your choice of paper or card or how you combine designs – as you make all these choices, your designs become unique and personal to you.

This book will show you what can be done, the tools and equipment that are available and some of the designs that are out there waiting to be discovered and turned into unique works of art. It will also show you how to look after your stamps so that they will last and continue to give you pleasure for a lifetime.

Once you have learnt the techniques, the only thing that will limit you is your imagination – so there is practically no limit at all.

The tools of the trade

Rubber stamping is one of those hobbies that can be as simple or as complicated as you want. You can just pick a few designs and use colour brush pens or a small ink pad and have great fun printing your own headed notepaper, wrapping paper and greeting cards. Or you can build up a collection of hundreds of rubber stamps; dozens of different ink pads and embossing pads; pots of clear, coloured, metallic and sparkling embossing powders; fancy edged scissors; special hand-made papers; card stock; glitter powder and embossing pens. The list continues to grow as more and more new products and catalogues arrive.

Although this book concentrates on papercraft, once you have mastered the art of rubber stamping you can go on to decorate almost anything. Fabric, walls, furniture, ceramics – all can be enhanced with this great craft. So, far from being a rather limited toy, your first rubber stamp can lead you to decorate and redesign almost anything in your home.

Rubber stamps

Where to find them

You will find a huge range of rubber stamps to choose from (see left), both the wood-mounted stamps, which will be the main type used in this book, and foam-backed sets.

Just browsing through the catalogues of a few companies can be a pleasant way to spend an evening. If you're lucky, you may live close to a specialist rubber stamp or craft shop, which means that you will have a good selection to choose from. Otherwise you may find that your local department store or art shop stocks a smaller selection, which is fine when you are just starting your collection but can be a bit limiting later. Many of the main suppliers and specialist shops also operate a mail-order service and you can find adverts for them in the various craft magazines.

A selection of wooden-block and foam-backed rubber stamps.

Inks

The term 'ink' covers a range of products that can be used to turn a rubber stamp into a printed image.

You can find a wide choice of single-coloured ink pads, rainbow-coloured ink pads, embossing pads, slow-drying pigment pads and embossing pens in almost any shop supplying rubber stamps.

For simple stamping projects, a quick-drying dye ink pad is ideal. They have a fairly thin ink which not only dries quickly but is also very good for printing with highly detailed rubber stamps, and things that get inked accidentally are easy to clean which makes them ideal for children. These ink pads come in a range of colours. Rainbow ink pads have three or five colours in one pad and give your work a multicoloured finish which is easy to achieve.

When you use rainbow pads, the first images that you print will have a distinct striped effect, but as you continue, the inks will run into one another and give a softer, more blended impression.

If you want to emboss your image, it must stay wet long enough for you to add the powder. Slow-drying embossing pads have very pale or clear ink; the colour of your finished work is supplied by the powder you use. You can also use slow-drying pigment ink pads for embossing. They come in many colours and in a range of rainbow pads (see above). The pads themselves are raised so that you can use them to ink the surface of large rubber stamps.

Rubber stamp art can also be enhanced by adding colour either directly on to the face of the rubber stamp or on to the printed image afterwards. The best way of doing this is to use the various brush pens that are available in art and craft shops and from rubber stamp suppliers. They are water-based and blend easily without leaving stripes in your work. The brush tip makes it easier to colour larger areas and many of these pens are dual tipped, with a fine tip for detailed work as well as the brush.

You can also buy embossing pens (see right). They have the same type of slow-drying ink as the embossing and pigment ink pads and you can use them to add lines, patterns, borders or messages to your design which can then

Ink pads come in a range of single colours, metallics and rainbows. Some are dye based, others are pigment ink pads.

A selection of brush pens and embossing pens.

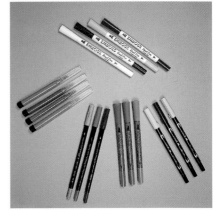

be embossed with embossing powder. They are available in various forms: fine line for basic writing, calligraphy tips, and brush tips for more free-form patterns. You can also buy them in coloured sets which can be embossed with clear powders.

Metallic, clear, coloured and sparkling embossing powders.

Embossing powder

Embossing powder sticks to an inked impression and melts when heated to give a raised 'embossed' finish.

You can find it in a wide range of colours and effects. Gold, silver, and clear – which enhances the colour of the pigment ink used – are the most popular, but once you have mastered the basics there are many more to choose from. You can have fun experimenting with vivid colours, metallic finishes, shimmering pearls, psychedelic colours, and embossing powders mixed with fine glitter which catch the light and look wonderful on projects such as Christmas cards (see left).

How to emboss an image

Whatever type of powder you use, the basic method for embossing remains the same:

1 Dab the rubber stamp lightly on the pigment ink pad a number of times to ensure an even covering of ink. If you are using a large rubber stamp, reverse the process and pat the ink pad across the face of the stamp.

2 Place the inked rubber stamp on the paper or card and press firmly and evenly on the back of the stamp but do not rock it as this will blur the image. Foam-backed rubber stamps require less pressure than wood-mounted stamps and care should be taken to ink only the raised image and not the rubber surround of these designs.

3 The embossing ink will stay wet long enough for you to add a second design or some freehand work with an embossing pen.

4 Once you have finished your design, cover it liberally with the embossing powder.

5 Remove any excess powder from the design or the surrounding paper or card by tapping the work firmly or by flicking it away with a soft brush. Some of the finer powders can even stick to fingerprints you leave on the paper and this excess powder must be removed or it will spoil your work. Don't worry about tapping the

work quite firmly, the powder will stick to the wet ink of your stamped image.

6   Tip the excess powder back into the container. You can do your embossing over a spare sheet of paper, pouring the powder from the pot it comes in and using the paper as a funnel to return it.

7   Melt the powder by heating the image. You can buy a special heating tool from your rubber stamp supplier, but, although they look similar, a hair dryer is not hot enough for this work. You can also use the heat from a toaster or hotplate by holding your work above the heat until the powder begins to melt. Whichever method you use, the powder will melt quite quickly and you should keep your work or the heat source moving to avoid burning the paper or card.

8   Once embossed, the design will cool rapidly and can be left as it is. Many designs do not need any further decoration, but if you do want to add colour, you can work with brush pens directly over the embossed image. The colour will not stick to the embossing, so the detail of the rubber stamp will still show through.

Once you have chosen your stamps you will want them to last, and with proper care they will last a lifetime. I have made thousands of impressions with some of my stamps and they still produce images as clear as they were the first time they were used.

Always clean your stamp when you have finished using it, to stop the ink drying into the design and clogging the detail. You can buy 'stamp cleaner', which is excellent; it is very easy and quick to use and will make your stamps look almost new (see right), but you can also use water to clean off the ink. Dampen a ball of cotton wool or a small sponge, squeeze the excess water from it and wipe the face of the stamp, pressing lightly into the more detailed areas where ink tends to stick.

Dry the surface carefully with some kitchen roll before you put the stamp away again. If you have used an ink which is particularly difficult to clean, such as black, gold or silver, you can use a little washing-up liquid in the water.

Never immerse the stamp in water or hold it under a running tap. The rubber will come away from the foam backing or wooden block and will be ruined.

Caring for your rubber stamps

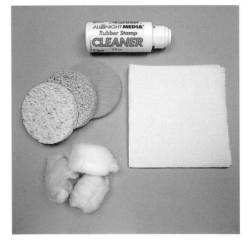

Cleaning equipment for a rubber stamp collection.

Once your rubber stamps are clean, store them carefully, away from direct sunlight. A shoe box or food storage box is ideal. Do not place the stamps on top of one another in storage because the pressure will damage the face of the stamp. Try standing them on their edge to fit more into the space.

Other tools and products

Glitters can be added to rubber stamp art with glue.

There are a number of other tools and products which you may find useful to add to your collection as you increase the range of your work.

Tinsel and glitter

Ultra-fine glitter can be added to your design using glue. It comes in a range of colours and is finer than the glitter and glitter glue that you can buy in stationery shops. It is particularly useful when you make children's birthday cards or Christmas cards (see left).

Liquid appliqué

This product adds an embroidered 3-D effect to paper or fabrics. It comes in a tube and can be used like a pen to draw your design or to add detail, such as leaves on a tree or the wool on a sheep. You must let it dry overnight before heating it to make the colour pop-up (see left).

Liquid appliqué adds a three-dimensional effect to a design.

Hand-made paper

You can now buy hand-made papers in many craft shops and they give an extra dimension to your rubber stamping (see left). Mulberry paper in particular can be very striking. It comes in beautiful colours

A range of coloured papers and hand-made mulberry papers.

such as burgundy, lavender, royal blue and salmon. When you tear it carefully, the fibres in the paper give a soft, feathered finish to your design.

Decorative scissors

Most people have come across zig-zag or pinking scissors, but there are now a number of different decorative scissors available. Deckle-edge scissors give the impression of a torn edge to your paper, but there are also a number of other designs such as scallop, wavy, Victorian or zig-zag. They are very useful for giving a decorative edge to a card or adding a decorative detail to one piece of a 3-D design.

Paper Edgers and Corner Edgers (supplied by Fiskars) give an interesting finish to a piece of work.

Craft knife and cutting mat

It is much easier to cut around small details with a craft knife than with scissors. You will find this type of knife in any craft or stationery shop and it is safer to choose one with a retractable blade which snaps to give new cutting tips. Most craft knives come with spare blades and you can buy new packs of blades as you need them. A self-healing cutting mat is also a very useful tool as it will save your table top from any unwanted carving and prevent your work or knife from slipping as you cut (see right).

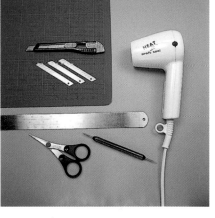

Glue

A wide range of glues is available. PVA adhesive is very useful for working with card and paper, as it dries clear and so does not spoil your work. Glue pens are also very clean and easy to use and they work especially well when you want to add glitter to a design.

Whichever glue you choose, it is important to pick one which will not damage or distort your work as it dries.

Useful tools: a heat tool, a metal rule, scissors, a craft knife and spare blades, a cutting mat and a scoring tool.

Tape

Many craft workers prefer double-sided sticky tape to glue; if used correctly it can hold just as fast, without showing and, of course, it is nowhere near as messy.

BASIC INKING

Project **Bookmark**

R ubber stamping is a very easy hobby to get started with. All you need to make your first piece of rubber stamp art is a rubber stamp and a quick-drying dye ink pad.

As you look around at the display of stamps in your local craft shop or flick through the pages of a rubber stamp company's catalogue, you will see what a huge range of designs there are to choose from. They range from simple flower motifs to highly detailed botanical prints, and famous cartoons to animal designs. There are even styles resembling finely detailed woodcuts (see right).

When buying your very first rubber stamp, try to pick a design that you will be able to use on all sorts of items. You may find one that suits one of your interests or obsessions. This is a way of being able to get real use out of the rubber stamp and therefore acquire the habit of using rubber stamp art. You will be able to personalise your letters and cards, print your own gift tags, put your mark on any new books that you buy and, of course, make bookmarks. And the chances are that anyone receiving a gift or letter from you bearing that stamp will know instantly who it's from; you'll have made that image your own.

A small selection of quick-drying, dye-based ink pads and small wood-mounted rubber stamps.

After you have chosen the rubber stamp design, you will need an ink pad to go with it. A quick-drying dye ink pad in a single colour is the easiest type to begin with, because you won't have to worry about the print smudging as it dries. That still gives you a very good range of colours and suppliers to choose from.

Deciding how to begin when confronted with your first rubber stamp, ink pad and an empty piece of card can be a little daunting. After all, nothing is more daunting than blank paper! A single design, printed on a sheet of card, can make a very effective piece of work, but you can create a more exciting and more original design by making multiple prints, especially if you are working with a small rubber stamp design.

For this project I have used a single maple leaf rubber stamp, and used this one design to build up a pattern of leaves on the bookmark.

Materials and equipment

Maple Leaf (© Rubber Stampede no. 272 D)
Crystal ink pad (© Rubber Stampede)
Packet of bookmarks and tassels
Sheet of plain paper
Rubber stamp cleaner and kitchen paper towel

Method

 STEP 1

Once you have gathered together your rubber stamp, ink pad, bookmark and paper, you are ready to ink the face of the rubber stamp. The aim is to get enough ink on the stamp face to make a clear impression, but not too much, because that will clog the detail. Place the rubber stamp gently on to the ink pad a few times until you feel that you have gathered enough ink. It is also important to be fairly careful to ink the actual design and not the surrounding surface, especially when you are using foam-backed rather than wood-mounted stamps.

Step 1 (a) Ink the face of the rubber stamp by pressing it firmly on to the ink pad.

Step 1 (b) The ink should cover but not clog the detail of the stamp design.

 STEP 2

There is a knack to getting good quality images from your rubber stamps, so it's best to try out your design on some plain paper first.

Place the inked rubber stamp flat on to the paper, firmly but gently, applying pressure evenly to the back of the pad.

When using a small rubber stamp design, you can get sufficient

even pressure with your fingertips, but with a larger block it is best to press with the palm of your hand. If you don't press firmly enough, the image will be too faint or you could miss parts of the design altogether, especially with a large rubber stamp. If you press too hard, the image will be smudged with too much ink, and you can also get some unwanted marks from the edge of the rubber or even the wooden block itself.

Do not rock the rubber stamp, because this will also smudge the image. Lift the stamp cleanly off the paper to leave a crisp impression.

These problems are easy to avoid with a little practice and you will quickly get a feel for how much pressure is just the right amount. Once you feel confident, you can move on to your bookmark.

Place the card on to a sheet of plain paper. This will enable you to make some images that fall off the edge of the bookmark without stamping your table.

 STEP 3 Build up your design by repeating the stamping process. There are no hard and fast rules as to how you should do this; the finished design is entirely up to you. The maple leaf design that I have used here works well as a rather informal design of falling leaves; some images are complete, while others consist of just the tips of the leaf. Other rubber stamp designs would suit a more formal approach.

Step 2 Make the first impression on the bookmark.

Step 3 Continue the pattern by making more, randomly placed images.

It is also possible to alter the effect by using a different coloured ink pad. For the maple leaves, I have chosen autumn colours of brown and red, but you could also use green for a much brighter effect, or even purple or bright pink if you really wanted to go wild.

The finished maple leaf bookmark printed in brown and red.

STEP 4

Once you have finished your artwork, it is very important to clean your rubber stamp. You should also do this before using another colour to prevent the colours mixing into an unpleasant shade of mud.

With the proper care, rubber stamps should last a lifetime and produce thousands of clear, sharp impressions for you, so it is well worth looking after them.

Clean the ink from the face of the rubber stamp. This will prevent a build-up of ink which would block and ultimately damage the rubber. You can use a stamp cleaner, which you can get from your rubber stamp supplier. Rub the soft top over the face of the stamp and then dry with a piece of kitchen roll or tissue. You can also use some cotton wool, either with plain water or a little liquid soap.

Do not use too much liquid soap or water and do not hold the rubber stamp under a tap or submerge it. This will damage your stamp and make the rubber lift from the block. Make sure that you dry your stamp after cleaning and store it away in a clean, dry place. Keep them away from strong sunlight or heat, as either can make the rubber shrink or crack. The best way to store your collection is in a small box, such as a shoe box, stacking each stamp on its side to prevent the design being squashed by the weight of other wooden blocks on top.

Step 4 Clean the face of the rubber stamp when you have finished.

Most of the rubber stamps that will be used in this book are wood-mounted blocks, but you can also find a good range of designs in foam-backed sets which are themed, such as butterflies, roses, a particular cartoon character or mini designs such as small fruit. You can also get sets for special events such as Christmas or birthday parties. The actual quality of the rubber stamp faces are the

A selection of foam-backed rubber stamps.

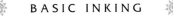
same as those mounted on wooden blocks and with a little care you can make prints of the same quality, but you do need to be aware of the main difference between the two types of mount: foam-backed stamps need to be inked much more carefully.

On a wood-mounted rubber stamp, the actual rubber and the foam it sits on is cut close to the design, so that the entire design is raised above the block. With a foam-backed stamp (see bottom left), the rubber is not cut away at the edge of the design, it forms the square or rectangle of the stamp block. It is very easy to ink this surround and end up with it forming part of your impression.

A badly inked stamp, with ink covering the rubber surround (left), compared with a well-inked example.

You have to take this into account when inking the rubber stamp (see above), and either keep the ink away from the edges or clean it off before making the impression. The Globe design has been badly inked – the ink has gone on to the surround and will print on the paper and spoil the work. The butterfly has been properly inked – the ink is lying on the design only – and will produce a clear print.

No matter how experienced you are, it is always a good idea to try a new rubber stamp on a spare piece of paper to see exactly how it will print, how much pressure it requires and if there are any areas of the block that you need to take care with. For instance, there may be a corner that needs slightly more pressure than the rest of the stamp. This can happen even if the underlying foam of the stamp is just a fraction uneven.

I have used a variety of rubber stamp designs to make the bookmarks shown on page 10.

The butterfly bookmark was printed using designs from a foam-backed rubber stamp set. The Smug Pig from Mostly Animals demonstrates how a single print can be used, and the Country Lane from Magenta creates a very ornate bookmark while still using the same simple printing technique of a single rubber stamp and a quick-drying ink pad, although it does require some experience.

PRINT EFFECTS

Project Jam labels

Home-made jam conjures up an image of a country kitchen, good old-fashioned food and the delicious scent of fruit simmering in the jam pan. What better way to finish off your special recipe than decorate the jars with your own labels?

It's much easier than you might think to create bright, coloured labels. Many of the rubber stamp collections feature designs for jam labels, others have border designs that you can use for the same purpose and, of course, you can also design your own using some small fruit and vegetable stamps.

Whatever design you choose, the basic technique that I have used for these labels is the same: you paint the actual rubber stamp design with water-based brush pens and use this to create the image.

First you must decide what design you want to use and what you are going to print on. You can use commercially available adhesive labels such as address labels, which you can find in a variety of sizes in any stationery or office supplies outlet. But if you do choose pre-cut labels, you must of course use a design that will fit on to them. If you decide to use paper and then cut out the finished print and glue it on to your jar, you have a much wider choice of design.

For this project, I have chosen a fruit border design which I will stamp on to some good-quality heavy paper – writing paper from your stationery shop is a good choice – and then cut out and glue on to the jars.

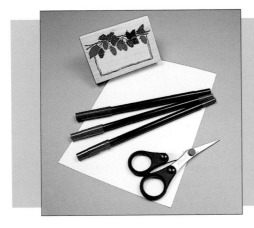

Materials and equipment

Raspberry label (© Rubber Stampede no. Z490F)
Art brush pens: purple, green and pink
Good-quality paper
Scissors, or craft knife and cutting mat
Glue
Rubber stamp cleaner, or cotton wool,
　　kitchen roll and water

Method

STEP 1

Gather your tools around you. Use good-quality brush pens rather than ordinary felt-tip pens, as they will stay wet longer. You can find this type of brush pen in most art and craft shops as well as from your rubber stamp supplier.

Choose two or three colours. Distinct colours are the easiest to work with, as they will stand out from one another. You have to work fairly quickly with this technique; there isn't time for detailed colouring.

STEP 2

Paint on to the face of your rubber stamp. Remember to cover the entire design. If you miss any part, such as the stalk of a berry, it will be missing when you make your print.

These are water-based colours, so when you have finished colouring you can refresh them by breathing across the stamp as if you were misting a window.

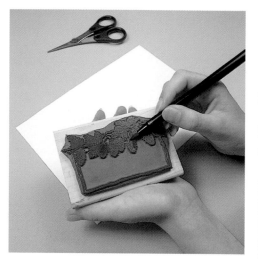

Step 2 Carefully colour the face of the rubber stamp with the brush pens.

Step 3 Press the rubber stamp firmly but gently on to the paper.

STEP 3

Press the rubber stamp firmly on to the paper, pressing down hard on the wooden block but not rocking the stamp, as this will cause blurring. Lift it off the paper cleanly.

STEP 4

If you want to make more labels, repeat steps 2–3. It will become easier to colour the stamp as you continue, because you will be able to see where you have added each colour before. Once you have printed as many labels as you want, carefully clean the ink from your stamp before you store it away.

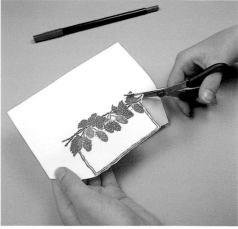

STEP 5

Cut carefully around your printed image to create each individual label. You can leave a small border or cut closely, whichever suits your own design. You now have your very own, designer jam label to finish off your home-made jam and of course you can also use design labels for marmalade, chutney or jars of dried herbs from your garden, or even your home-made wine.

Step 5 Cut around the printed image to create the label.

The finished label, glued on to the jar of jam.

Once you have mastered this technique of colouring the face of the rubber stamp, you can use it for all sorts of applications. Practise with some of your stamps to see the effects that you can achieve.

If you use the right colours, you can create work that looks as if it has been professionally printed. You can colour cartoon figures in the colours you would find in a book or film and create your own cartoon birthday card or cartoon strip.

Alternatively you can let your imagination run riot and end up with blue roses, red leaves, a purple sun, and pink cats and dogs.

RAINBOW EFFECTS

Project Wrapping paper

Beautiful wrapping paper can make any present seem special, and when you've taken the time to make the paper yourself it really does become the perfect finishing touch.

You can use almost any type of plain paper as your starting point, picking paper that will suit the present or the person you are giving it to: delicate tissue paper for a wedding gift, brown paper or the latest coloured craft papers for a larger present that requires a stronger wrapping, a sheet of basic, white, photocopy paper for a small gift or wall-lining paper for that really large, difficult-to-wrap present.

Of course, you can also pick a rubber stamp design that will match the gift, the event, or the person you are giving it to, or you can design your very own, individual paper and use it for all the gifts you give, making it a really personal finish.

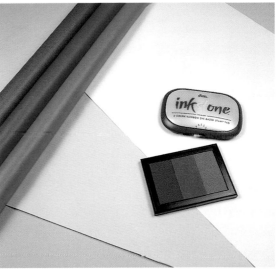

When using a rainbow ink pad, the choice of paper is important. There are many to choose from.

Once you have picked your base paper and the rubber stamp design, the final piece of equipment needed to help you to create a colourful and effective sheet of wrapping paper quickly and easily is a rainbow-coloured ink pad. Up until now, you have used a single-colour ink pad or put colour directly on to the face of the design. The main challenge with something as large as a sheet of wrapping paper is to make it look effective without it taking too long to print. This normally involves applying more than one colour. A quick-drying, rainbow-coloured ink pad does exactly that.

Materials and equipment

Strawberries (© Rubber Stampede no. A1585H)
Rainbow-coloured dye ink pad
A3 sheet of white paper

Method

STEP 1

Once you have selected the base paper and the rainbow ink pad that you are going to use, you can begin to ink the face of the rubber stamp.

At first, a new rainbow ink pad will produce a distinctly striped effect in the design. In this case, the blue, pink and purple can be seen clearly on the face of the inked stamp and in the prints that have already been made.

The effect will be even more noticeable if you use a pad with a bold combination of colours such as red, yellow and blue rather than a graduation of one colour such as shades of green, or pink to purple. Eventually, with use, the colours will merge and produce a more subtle effect, even if you use an ink pad with strong colours.

If you prefer to keep the colours distinct, be careful to reposition the rubber stamp on the same area of the ink pad each time. On the other hand, if you like the more shaded effect you can speed up the process by using your rubber stamp to smudge the ink between the different sections of the pad. Try not to be too vicious with this, and try to avoid altering the direction of the stamp, by putting the previously red-inked section of the design on to the blue part of the ink pad and vice versa, as you will end up with a sludge-coloured ink pad!

Step 1 The different coloured inks on the rainbow ink pad show clearly on the face of the the rubber stamp.

Step 2 Make repeat prints on the paper, re-inking for each print.

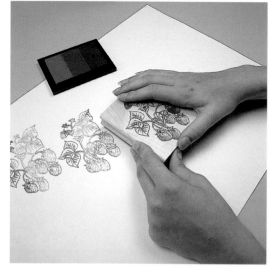

STEP 2

The technique that was used to obtain an informal, repeat pattern on the bookmark in Chapter 2 can be used again here on a larger scale. A design that sticks rigidly to the edges of a sheet of paper can look very stiff, so place a piece of spare paper under the paper you are working on and let some of the prints fall off the edge of your work and, rather than printing in straight lines, try a diagonal pattern across the paper.

The rainbow ink, repeated over the pattern, will quickly begin to produce a lively and colourful effect in your printing.

STEP 3

Repeat steps 1 and 2, inking and stamping your design until the sheet of paper is complete. If you stamp the design close together you will have a very colourful effect, while if you decide to leave more space between the individual designs you will retain more of the background colour of your paper.

STEP 4

Complete your designer wrapping paper by making a matching gift tag. Simply cut a piece of plain card the size you want to make your tag. Cut a section of your paper to the same size. Glue them together and leave to dry. When the tag is dry, punch a hole in one corner, thread a piece of ribbon through it and attach the gift tag to the parcel.

The finished paper, printed with two different rainbow ink pads.

You can also achieve different effects with the same rubber stamp and paper but by using different rainbow ink pads (see right). As you can see, the red, yellow and green ink pad has produced a stronger finish than the blue, pink and purple one.

Completely individual papers can be created, depending on how you combine colours and papers. Gold ink on a darker craft paper can look very striking, especially if you use a more solid rubber stamp design, such as the Sunflower Mosaic that I printed with gold on dark blue craft paper (see page 20).

You can also use two different ink pads rather than one rainbow pad to create your design. The gold Happy Anniversary stamp (© Rubber Stampede no. 2600E) combines well with the red Cascading Hearts (© Inca no. 601–A) when printed on white tissue paper (see page 20).

If you leave your printing more widely spaced, as with the rose spray, the background paper – in this case yellow craft paper – will be a stronger element in the finished design.

EMBOSSING I

Project Moving house notice

There are times when it would be marvellous to be able to announce special news to family and friends with professionally printed stationery. Unfortunately, professional printing is not economically viable for a small number of items.

Moving to a new home is one such event. You have to send out your new address and telephone number, but the quantity of cards you require would normally restrict you to a standard pad of forms from the stationery department. The craft of rubber stamping can solve this problem and in this project you will learn the technique of embossing.

Embossing is an extension of the printing techniques that we have already covered. In the place of the quick-drying dye ink pads, we will be using a slow-drying pigment ink and clear embossing powder.

The powder sticks to the wet ink and, when heated, melts to form a hard, glossy, raised surface, very similar to the effect you can get from professional printing.

The powder can be embossed by heating the stamped card or paper over a toaster, a hot plate or even a light bulb, but a heat tool, readily available from most rubber stamp suppliers, makes the task much quicker and easier.

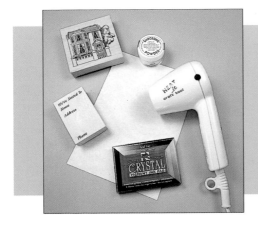

Materials and equipment

House (© Superstamp no. G6217)
We've Moved (© Superstamp no. D6216)
Green pigment ink pad
Sheet of card
Clear embossing powder
Heat tool

Method

STEP 1

The rubber stamps for this project are larger than some of the ones we have used in earlier projects, so the method of inking is slightly different.

Instead of putting the stamps down on to the ink pad, this time hold the rubber stamp in one hand, the ink pad in the other, and ink on to the face of the stamp. As you can see, the slow-drying pigment pads are raised off the base, rather than being set flat into a plastic case, and this makes it easier to ink larger rubber stamps.

Step 1 The raised face of the pigment pad makes it easy to ink a large rubber stamp.

STEP 2

Take a sheet of plain white paper and crease it down the middle before placing your card over it. You will use this to catch the excess embossing powder later. Make the impression of the house on your card and repeat the inking and stamping process with the We've Moved stamp. The ink is specially designed to be slow drying, giving you time to work on a design with more than one stamp before adding the embossing powder.

STEP 3

Once you have made both impressions, pour the clear embossing powder over the entire design. Use plenty of powder to cover the wet ink. Don't worry about using too much powder, it will only stick to the wet ink, any spare will easily fall off the card when you lift it. Tap the edge of the card lightly against the paper to remove the last traces of powder.

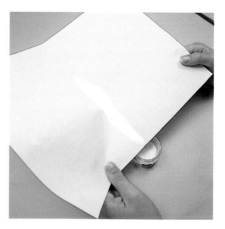

Step 3 Cover the entire surface of the image with the embossing powder.

Step 4 Return the excess powder to the pot for future use.

STEP 4

Set the powdered card to one side and carefully fold the paper into the crease that was formed earlier. Use this as a funnel to return the excess powder to the pot. This can be used again later.

Step 5 Melt the embossing powder with a heat tool.

STEP 5

Use your heat tool to gently heat the powder. Experiment a little until you get the feel of the tool. Hold the nozzle about 3–6in (7.5–15cm) from the card. As the powder heats you can actually see it melting. It turns from a grainy covering – which dulls the colour of the ink – to a glossy, highly coloured sheen.

If you go too close you will singe the paper or card; if you don't go close enough the powder will not melt. The distance will also vary with the type of embossing powder and paper that you are using. Some powders melt more quickly, while all powders will emboss faster when you use paper rather than card.

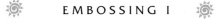

STEP 6

Cut the card to the size you require, remembering to leave enough space to write your new name and address clearly.

Once you have mastered the embossing technique, it will form the basis of much of your rubber stamp art. It creates a much more professional and permanent image for your work.

Pigment inks are available in a wide range of colours – vivid, subtle, pale and dark – and clear embossing powder will bring out the colour and make it look richer.

Although you can also buy a wide variety of coloured embossing powders – in which your finished work is the colour of the powder rather than the ink – it is probably best to start with coloured pigment ink pads and clear embossing powder. In this way, you can vary the colour of your printing simply by purchasing a new ink pad.

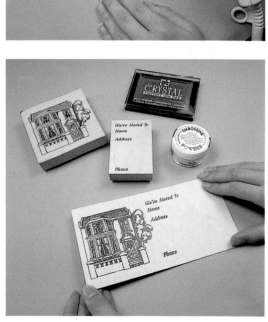

Step 6 The finished card, cut to the required size.

EMBOSSING II

Project **Gift box**

A hand-made gift box can make the smallest present special, and it's far easier to make than it looks. You can buy preformed gift boxes ready to decorate from various rubber stamp companies. They come in a number of shapes: pillow boxes, pyramids, petal boxes, and, of course, cubes. But for this project we are going to start with a sheet of card.

The card needs to be thin enough to crease and fold easily but thick enough to make a box that will be sufficiently strong to safely hold your gift. Look for card that is between 160–250gsm in weight. You can buy packs of between four and twelve sheets of A4 card in various colours, including metallics, from most stationery shops.

We will also be using an embossing pad and gold embossing powder for the first time, which gives a very rich, opulent feel to a piece of work – just right for a gift box.

When you are making an item that has to be folded, you can simply crease the card by pressing along the line with your thumb, but it is much easier and produces a crisper finish if you score the line of the fold first. You can do this with a scoring or embossing tool which you should be able to get from your rubber stamp supplier or a local craft shop. In this case 'embossing' refers to the technique of putting a line or pattern on to card by pressing with a round-edged tool, rather than the kind of embossing with powder and heat that we use in rubber stamp art.

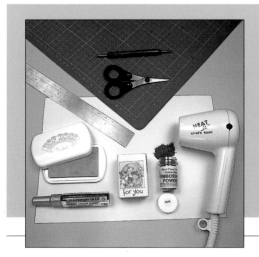

Materials and equipment

A4 sheet of 160gsm white card
For You (© Funstamps no. M-FF-304)
Embossing ink pad
Gold embossing powder
Heat tool
Self-healing cutting mat, scissors, metal rule and
    scoring tool
Glue pen

Method

STEP 1

Use a photocopier or tracing paper to transfer the box template (see page 36) on to your sheet of card. You can enlarge the design and use a larger sheet of card if you want to make a bigger box. A detailed explanation of how to make several styles of gift boxes is included at the end of this chapter.

STEP 2

Cut out your box pattern carefully, making sure that you only cut the solid lines, not the dotted fold lines.

STEP 3

Place the card on to your cutting mat and, using a metal rule to keep a straight line, score the fold lines to help the finished box fold neatly. Some people prefer to score the fold lines before they cut out the pattern. After a number of goes, you'll find a way that suits you best.

Step 4 Place each impression on to the correct section of the box.

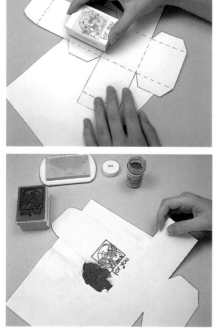

STEP 4

Stamp the design on to the card. If you have drawn the lines with a soft pencil, they can be rubbed out after you have finished your printing. But if you have drawn them with pen, used carbon paper or photocopied the lines on to your card, it's a good idea to stamp on to the other side and use that as the face of your box so that the design won't be spoilt by ugly marks.

Ink from an embossing pad is normally blue or pink, but so pale that it is almost colourless. This can make it difficult to see your design when you have stamped it. But don't worry, the powder will stick to it!

For this box I have chosen a design with words as well as a picture, so it is especially important to make sure that each print will be the right way up when you have stuck the box together. A little time taken to work it out at this stage will save you from having to start all over again.

Step 5 Cover the impression with gold embossing powder.

STEP 5

Pour the gold embossing powder over the design, making sure that you cover all your printing. At this stage the powder is a rather dull, dirty colour but it will melt into a beautiful glowing gold.

The embossing ink is clear, so any mistakes that you may have made in making the print, such as catching the corner of the block or making a mark with the edge of the rubber, can be removed at this stage: simply remove the powder carefully from the area. Use a small, soft paint brush to do this without damaging the rest of your print.

Step 6 Use the heat tool to melt the powder.

Use the heat tool to melt the embossing powder. As it melts, you will be able to see it rising off the card and turning into a rich golden sheen. It will take a few moments to cool, so it is best to avoid touching it or placing it face down at first.

Continue with steps 4–6 until you have completed your design on all sides of the box.

Once it has cooled, fold the box carefully along the scored lines. If you do this before printing, the embossing powder may collect in the creases and spoil your design. It is easier to make all the folds first before you begin gluing any of the tabs. Use a paper glue that will dry to a clear finish. A glue pen, which goes on blue but dries clear, is ideal, because it is easy to position cleanly.

The finished box is ideal for small gifts, such as chocolates, or even a couple of rubber stamps!

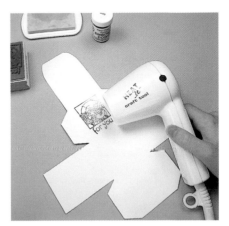

Step 8 Make all folds in the box first and then glue the tabs into place.

The finished box. Remember to leave the top unglued so that you can put the gift inside!

Once you have mastered this technique, there are all sorts of beautiful embossing powders that you can use. Gold is striking and luxuriant, of course, but you can also use silver, copper and bronze. You could also experiment with bright primary-coloured powders, special effects such as verdigris and powders that have a glitter or sparkling finish, such as white glitter which can look like snow. Clear sparkling powders bring out the colour of the embossing ink, while hologram powder makes your design change colour as the light hits it. The effects that you can achieve are almost endless and there are always new colours being launched for you to add to your collection.

You can also achieve different effects by using coloured card for your box, as I did with the red cube box decorated with a gold Cascading Heart design from Inca (see page 28).

The pyramid box was printed with verdigris embossing powder, using designs from a foam-backed set of travel stamps from All Night Media, while the pillow box was printed with a set of foam-backed stamps and copper powder.

Making gift boxes

Cube box

The boxes shown in these drawings are larger than those shown in the photographs. This is so that you can see clearly what is being done at each step.

1. Transfer the template (see page 36) on to your chosen card. Cut around the solid lines.
2. Score the dotted lines using a scoring tool and a metal rule.

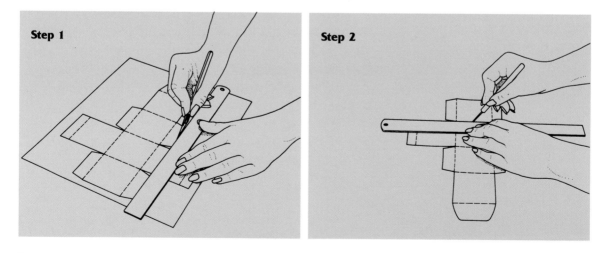

Step 1

Step 2

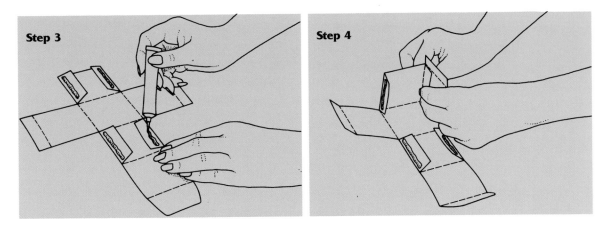

3. When you have completed the printing, make all the folds of the box inwards and add glue to the tabs.

4. Stick the box together, remembering to leave the top of the box unstuck.

Pyramid box

1. Transfer the template (see page 37) on to your chosen card. Once again, begin by cutting around the solid lines and scoring along the dotted lines. Then make the holes at the top of the two sides, as shown in the template.

2. When you have completed the printing, make all the folds of the box inwards.

3. Add glue to tabs B and C. Fold up three sides and stick the tabs together.

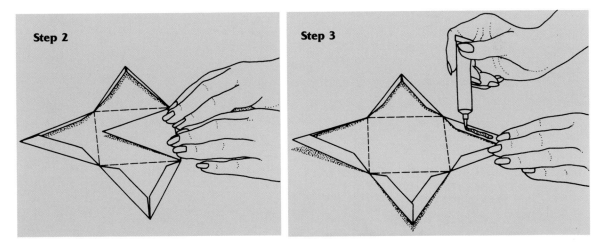

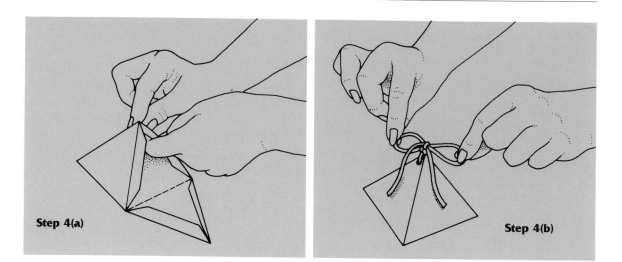

Step 4(a)

Step 4(b)

4(a) and (b). You now have one side free. When you have put the gift inside the box, bring up this last side and secure it to its opposite side with string or ribbon running through the two holes. Alternatively, you may decide not to glue the box together at all, in which case make a hole in the top of each of the four sides and tie them together.

Pillow box

1. Transfer the template (see page 38) on to your chosen card. Cut around the solid lines and score along the dotted lines (you may need to use a saucer or some other curved object as a guide when scoring the curved lines).

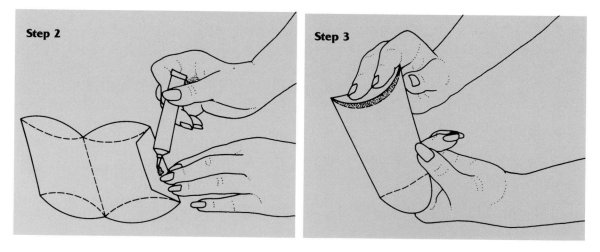

Step 2

Step 3

2. After printing, fold in the flap and put glue on the reverse side. Then, stick the flap to the inside of the opposite panel.

3. Fold in the end panels. As you do so the box will expand into a pillow shape and the ends will become concave. No glue is necessary but you may wish to put a dab between the end panels to prevent the box from being opened prematurely.

Four-petal box

1. Transfer the template (see page 39) on to your chosen card. Cut around the solid lines and score along the dotted lines.

2. Fold over the tabs and put some glue on to the reverse side of each one.

3. Bring up all four sides of the box and stick the tabs to the inside of the panels they come to meet.

4. Fold over the four petals, one by one, in an anti-clockwise direction. Tuck the last petal underneath the first.

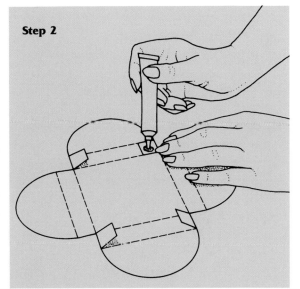

Step 2

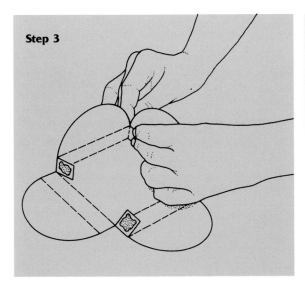

Step 3

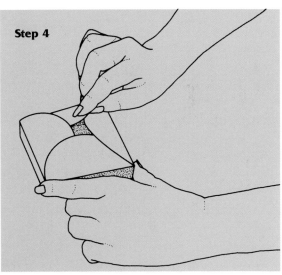

Step 4

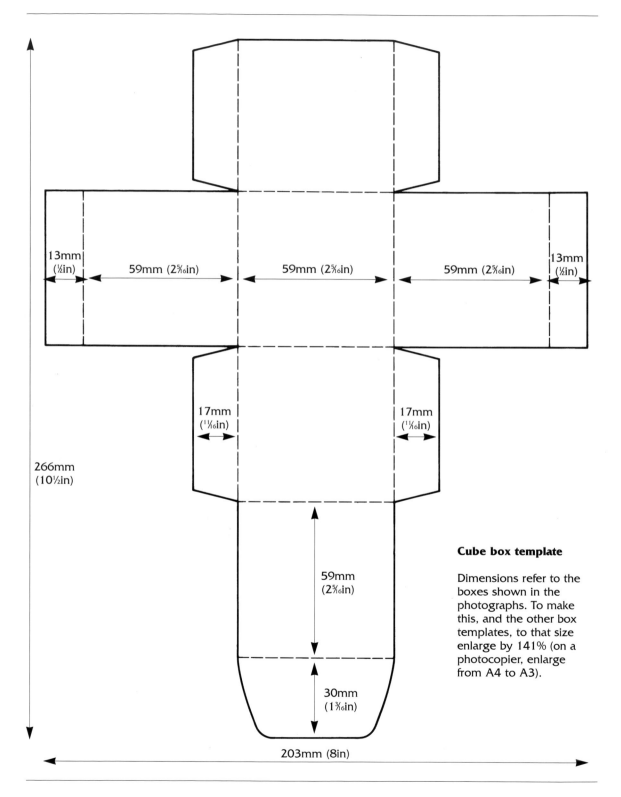

13mm (½in)

59mm (2⅜in)

59mm (2⅜in)

59mm (2⅜in)

13mm (½in)

17mm (¹¹⁄₁₆in)

17mm (¹¹⁄₁₆in)

266mm (10½in)

59mm (2⅜in)

30mm (1³⁄₁₆in)

203mm (8in)

Cube box template

Dimensions refer to the boxes shown in the photographs. To make this, and the other box templates, to that size enlarge by 141% (on a photocopier, enlarge from A4 to A3).

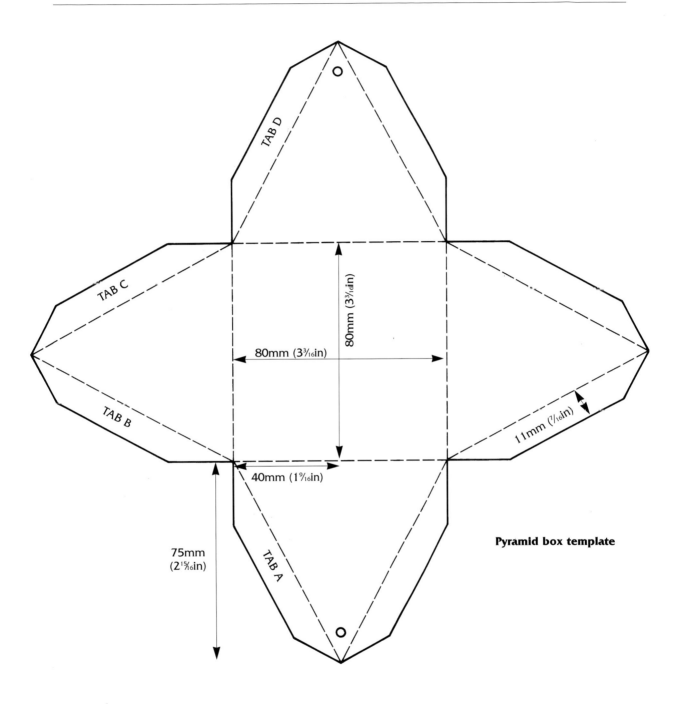

TAB D

TAB C

TAB B

TAB A

80mm (3³/₁₆in)

80mm (3³/₁₆in)

11mm (⁷/₁₆in)

40mm (1⁹/₁₆in)

75mm
(2¹⁵/₁₆in)

Pyramid box template

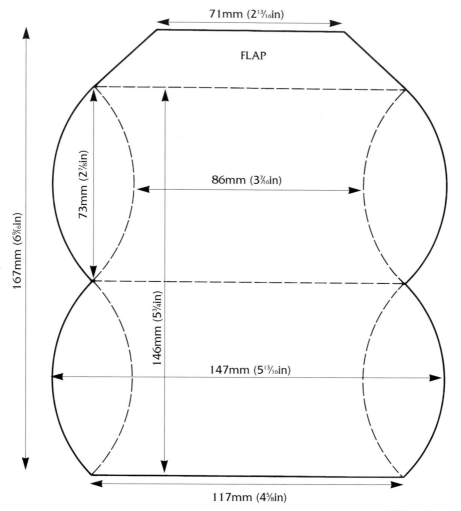

71mm (2¹³⁄₁₆in)

FLAP

167mm (6⁹⁄₁₆in)

73mm (2⁷⁄₈in)

86mm (3⁷⁄₁₆in)

146mm (5³⁄₄in)

147mm (5¹³⁄₁₆in)

117mm (4⁵⁄₈in)

Pillow box template

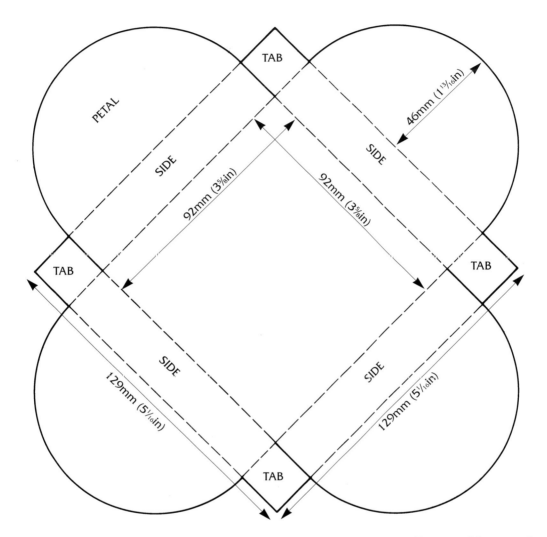

Four-petal box template

Dimensions refer to the boxes shown in the photographs. To make this, and the other box templates, to that size enlarge by 141% (on a photocopier, enlarge from A4 to A3).

COMBINING
TECHNIQUES I

Project **Stationery**

Hand-made stationery can make letter writing a pleasure and in this project I have employed the embossing technique that you have already seen, again with clear powder, but this time with a slow-drying pigment rainbow pad. This will help you to produce a professionally printed effect on a larger number of items in a fairly short time – just what you need when you are printing writing paper and matching envelopes.

You can achieve all sorts of effects depending on what materials you begin with. Pigment rainbow pads come in an even larger range of colour combinations than the dye-based variety, and you can pick from three-colour, five-colour and even eight-colour combinations.

As these are slow-drying pigment inks, you have plenty of time to use two or three different rubber stamps to produce the design you want before having to add the embossing powder. In this project I have used two rubber stamps, but have made a number of impressions with each stamp to create the final design.

A selection of different papers and matching envelopes with rainbow pigment pads and rubber stamp designs.

The variety of papers now available in stationery outlets as well as from your craft shop or rubber stamp supplier will also help you to create different effects. Classic laid papers, papers with bright colours or marble effects, and even hand-made papers are readily available, with matching envelopes and sometimes even matching folders in which to keep your completed work. Of course, you can also turn ordinary white paper and envelopes into your very own work of art.

It is best to use a heavier, good-quality paper, because embossing can bleed through to the back of thinner paper and spoil the effect of your work. Try out the technique on a few different types of paper before you make your final choice.

Not only is your own stationery a joy to have and fun to create, it can make the perfect gift for someone who likes writing letters. It's unique, it can be designed to suit the person – flowers for a gardener, a musical design for a singer – and it's that most treasured of gifts, one that you have put your time into.

Materials and equipment

Harvest Corner (© First Class Stamps no. X10F)
Harvest Border (© First Class Stamps no. X11E)
Rainbow pigment pad
Clear embossing powder
Writing paper and envelopes
Heat tool

Method

STEP 1

Once you have selected your paper, rubber stamp designs and rainbow colours, it is important to decide how you are going to turn the individual rubber stamps into a design. Try out your design on a spare piece of paper first and test how the different rubber stamps work together.

In this example, the Harvest Border and Harvest Corner stamps are from the same company and indeed are from the same collection, so they combine very easily, the flowers from both designs flowing into each other. But you may have chosen rubber stamps from different collections to achieve the design you want, so it is best to work with them first before you move on to your more expensive paper.

Step 2 Plan the flow of the colours on the paper.

STEP 2

As you are using smaller rubber stamps again for this project, you ink them by placing the rubber stamp on to the pad, using the same techniques as those you learnt in Chapter 4 to either keep the colours separate or blend them together.

When you are adding a second or third impression to your design, do remember to decide first whether you want the different colours to flow into each other or be sharply divided.

In this design, I matched the blue end of the Harvest Border to the blue side of the Harvest Corner and the red to the red so that the colours flowed across the page.

STEP 3

Once you have completed the design on a single piece of paper, cover it with clear embossing powder. Remove the excess and return it to the pot.

STEP 4

Melt the powder with the heat tool. You will find that the powder melts more quickly on paper than it does on heavier sheets of card.

STEP 5

Continue with steps 2–4 until you have produced as many sheets as you require. You can print and add powder to three or four sheets, removing the excess powder from each as you go, before actually melting the powder to complete the embossing process.

Step 4 Heat the embossing powder.

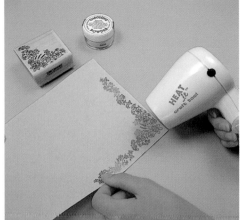

If you do work this way, take care not to brush the powder from the design before you apply the heat and avoid piling the newly melted sheets directly on top of one another, because they could stick together!

Do not be tempted to print all your stationery before heating the embossing powder; the powder will fall away from the design if the ink dries out.

STEP 6

Once you have your writing paper, decide how you would like to decorate your matching envelopes. Obviously you will want to either use the same or a complementary design, and the same colour combinations of ink and paper, but you must remember to leave space for writing an address and stamping the finished letter. In this design I just used the Harvest Corner stamp in the bottom left-hand corner of the envelope (see right). It is advisable to keep your design in this position if you want to send your envelopes through the postal system.

The finished paper and its matching envelope.

Although I have used a rainbow pigment pad for this project and for the musical design (see page 40), you can also achieve a very dramatic design with a single colour, especially when you use the colour of your paper as part of the design.

The coffee-coloured paper combines perfectly with brown ink to create the coffee beans design, while a bright orange paper provides the colour interest for the black cat design.

HAND PAINTING
AN EMBOSSED
DESIGN

Project **Recipe card**

So far, we have used the colours from inks and embossing powders to enhance the design of the rubber stamps, but you can also add colour to the finished print.

The raised nature of the embossed outline makes painting or colouring the design very simple. The actual embossing, whether you have used clear or coloured embossing powders, will repel any paint, leaving the details of the rubber stamp raised above any colour that is added to the design. For instance, the veins of a leaf will still show clearly when you go over the entire inside area with a green brush pen. It is also very easy to keep your colour inside the lines of the design when you can actually feel the line of embossing with your pen!

The brush pens that you can find in a craft shop or from your rubber stamp supplier are the best way to colour your stamp art. They are more like watercolour paints than ordinary felt-tip pens and they do not leave stripes in your colouring. You can buy them in sets, or individually, in a very wide range of colours, and many of them are dual ended, with a fine tip as well as a brush point.

This technique again opens up a completely new area for your rubber stamp art. The fact that you choose the colours and the combinations of colour for each design will help to make each print unique to you.

In the same way that a single rubber stamp or a collection of designs can be used to produce a set of stationery, a suitable food or kitchen design can be used on a card index system to give an individual look to a personal collection of special or favourite recipes. You could also decorate the card index box or file to match, and design a special set for a friend who has a passion for cooking rather than rubber stamping!

The design in black pigment ink, embossed with clear powder.

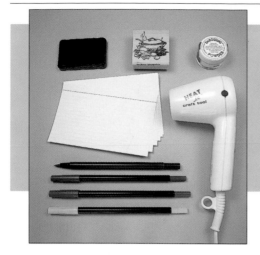

Materials and equipment

Garden Goodies (© Funstamps no. F-F21)
Black pigment pad
Clear embossing powder
Index cards
Brush pens: green, yellow, red, orange, brown
Heat tool

Method

STEP 1

For this project I have used black pigment ink and clear embossing powder, because it is the colour that is added after the printing that is important in this design.

Ink your rubber stamp with the black ink pad and make the impression on the index card.

STEP 2

Cover the design with clear embossing powder and remove the excess, returning it to the pot.

STEP 3

Melt the embossing powder with the heat tool.

STEP 4

When you have printed and embossed the number of recipe cards that you want at this stage, start to colour the design. You can colour them all identically or you could decide to create a colour coding system: red casserole pots for stews, yellow for finger food, or pink for sweets and desserts.

When you are colouring, you can draw your pen straight across the full area. For instance, with the carrots, you don't have to worry about the small black lines of shaping, and with the actual pot you need not worry about the division between the base and the lid. These embossed details will reject the ink from your pen and will show through clearly in your finished work.

Good-quality brush pens are an investment. They produce a high-quality finish and you should take care of them. The brush point will bend and flow to an extent, almost like a paint brush, but do not press too hard with it or you will damage it permanently.

Always remember to replace the lid at once to stop the pen drying out and take care if painting over another colour as this will stain the brush. This is especially so with lighter-coloured pens, such as yellow or pale pink.

If you enjoy creating this type of rubber stamp art, you will find that certain types of rubber stamp design are more suitable than others for adding colour. It is better to avoid designs with very large empty areas inside the design. They take a lot of colour and can still end up looking rather flat. At the other extreme, designs with a great deal of detail can also be spoilt by adding extra colour, it is often better to paint the actual face of this type of design instead, as we did with the jam labels in Chapter 3.

Don't worry too much; you will find hundreds and hundreds of rubber stamp designs that look wonderful when coloured!

Step 4 Colour over the embossed design. The embossing will repel the coloured inks from the brush pen.

The finished card with the recipe added.

EMBOSSING AND
HAND PAINTING

Project **Wedding invitation**

In this project I have used embossing and then hand colouring to create a design in the same way as the recipe card in Chapter 8, but this time I have used silver embossing powder and added some ultra-fine glitter powder after painting to give the design some sparkle.

Ultra-fine glitter powders are available in an increasing palette of colours. The very subtle opalescent that I chose for this project is perfect for wedding stationery, either on its own or over a colour, where it allows the underlying colour to shine through. You can also buy glitters that have a colour of their own: very pale ones, such as lemon or pink, right through the spectrum to vivid blues and bright reds, as well as metallics, such as gold and copper.

The ultra-fine glitter powders that are supplied by rubber stamp companies and some craft shops are very different to the tubes of glitter and glitter glue available in stationery or toy departments. Some of the ultra-fine glitters are so fine that they are almost dust and they catch and reflect the light as it falls on your work. The standard glitters can be used on rubber stamp art but you must take care to match the type of glitter to the kind of work you are creating.

In order to create a range of wedding stationery, I have employed a single rubber stamp to establish an overall design but adapted it by using a selection of rubber stamps with different wording. In this way, I have created a wedding invitation, an evening invitation, an Order of Service, a thank you card and a menu. A number of companies have a very good range of wording stamps for special events, such as weddings, family birthdays, special wedding anniversaries and, of course, Christmas, New Year, Easter and other holidays.

You can buy packs of blank cards and envelopes from most craft shops and if you want larger quantities, your rubber stamp supplier should be able to help you.

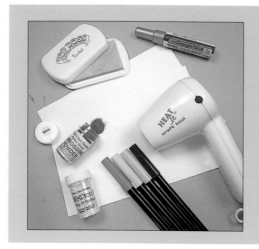

Materials and equipment

Heart and Flowers (© All Night Media no. 388F)
Wedding Invitation, Evening Invitation, Order of
    Service, Thank You, Menu (© Stamps Unlimited)
White A5 card, creased
Silver embossing powder
Embossing ink pad
Heat tool
Brush pens
Opalescent ultra-fine glitter
Glue pen

Method

Step 1 The set of rubber stamp designs required to make the complete range of wedding stationery.

 STEP 1

It is important that your collection has the same overall 'feel' throughout. The main rubber stamp will obviously help this, but the other stamp designs must be considered as well.

Plan your layout before you actually start to print on to your card stock. Make sure that you have taken the different wordings into account. A style that will suit your wedding invitation may not leave enough room to print 'Order of Service'. Once you are happy with your overall concept you can begin printing.

STEP 2

Ink the rubber stamp that forms your main design and make an impression on the card. Then ink the wording rubber stamp for this set and add it to the design.

STEP 3

Cover the card with silver embossing powder and remove the excess, returning it to the pot.

STEP 4

Emboss the design with your heat tool. The rather dull grey powder will melt into a beautiful liquid silver as you apply the heat.

STEP 5

Repeat steps 2, 3 and 4 until you have completed the first set. Then change your wording stamp for the next one required. Continue until you have printed your entire range.

STEP 6

Once you have your complete range of stationery, you can begin to add colour to the design. It is easier to complete the printing process first and then clean and store your rubber stamps before going on to this stage. Select the colours you want to use from your brush pens. The fact that your stationery is all hand-printed means that you can match it to the colour scheme of the wedding itself, so do take this into account when you choose your pens.

Step 4 Melt the powder with a heat tool to create the raised silver effect.

Step 6 Add colour to the design with brush pens.

Step 7 Use a glue pen carefully to cover the area that will take the glitter.

The very wide range of colours and shades now available in brush pens (some ranges have over 140 colours) means that you can match almost any colour scheme. It is well worth planning all the details of such a project in advance and ordering the brush pens specifically.

 Now that the design is coloured, you can begin to add the ultra-fine glitter. You will find that this can really make the card come alive and it will certainly make your stationery look special. Using a glue pen, add the glue to the section of the design you want to highlight with glitter.

You can draw with a glue pen almost as you would with a felt-tip pen. This allows you to place your glue and therefore your glitter very accurately.

 Add the glitter to the wet glue immediately, treating the ultra-fine glitter in the same way as you do embossing powder, removing the excess and returning it to the pot each time.

Decorate all of your designs following steps 6, 7 and 8 until you have completed your stationery collection.

Step 8 Sprinkle the glitter powder over the glued areas.

Once you have the covers, you can produce the middle sections of your cards. These will include the actual invitation details, the words of the hymns for the Order of Service, or your thank you message. Cut your insert paper slightly smaller than the card size so that it does not show when the card is folded.

Print the words on a computer, photocopy them, or write them using calligraphy and attach them to the inside of the card with glue.

Ultra-fine glitter can make a pretty card into a beautiful card, but it must be used with the right type of rubber stamp design. The heart that I have used for this collection is an obvious choice for highlighting with glitter powder, and some other rubber stamp designs, such as the champagne glasses on the evening invitation (see page 48), are also suitable. With others you have to be a bit more imaginative, as with the light shining through the stained glass windows on the wedding invitation.

The finished range of wedding stationery.

Make sure that the glitter will add to the design you have chosen; don't force it on to an inappropriate piece of artwork. I have not added any to the church design or to the bride and groom.

The more vividly coloured glitters are easier to use in smaller areas. On large designs, you should colour the area first in the same shade; any tiny gaps in the glitter will look very obvious when the pale background shows through.

The range of colours available is continually expanding and the technique can be used to add excitement, glamour or elegance to many types of work. You can have a clutch of multicoloured balloons for a birthday card, a champagne glass full of sparkling champagne for an anniversary celebration or shining bows on a Christmas tree – the choice is yours.

USING
LIQUID APPLIQUÉ

Project **Gift tag**

As you are beginning to see, there are many different products available to enhance your rubber stamp artwork, and many different things that you can make with them. The only real limit is your imagination!

In this project I will show you how a very simple image can be enhanced by using a product called liquid appliqué. This can be used on fabrics as well as card, so you may be able to find it in a haberdashery department as well as at your normal suppliers. It comes in pen form and runs smoothly from the nib, like a thick ink.

When liquid appliqué is heated, it bubbles up from the surface, creating a 3-D effect on your work. It is ideal for adding a snow effect to Christmas tags, fluffy rabbit tails, bobbles to hats or leaves to a tree design. For this project I have used it to add a rich centre to a sunflower.

The gift tags that you find in the shops can be very boring, and it's almost impossible to find one that bears any relation to the gift that you are giving or the person you're giving it to. They are so easy to make that once you have started you may never buy one again. Of course, you can also match the tag to the wrapping paper or gift box that you have made; you could even match it to your greetings card.

A number of rubber stamp companies sell packets of gift tags, some in a variety of shapes and others with their own small envelopes. It's easy to make your own, however, and at the end of this project you will find some shapes to trace or photocopy on to your own choice of card.

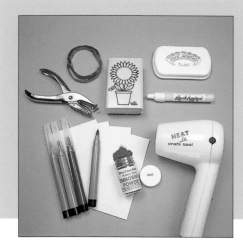

Materials and equipment

Sunflower (© Personal Impressions no. 139M)
A gift tag or, if you prefer to make your own, card,
    scissors and a hole punch
Embossing ink pad
Gold embossing powder
Brush pens
Yellow liquid appliqué
Heat tool
Ribbon

Method

 STEP 1
If you are going to make your own gift tags from sheets of card, trace or copy the design and cut it out. Otherwise, simply take a tag from the packet.

 STEP 2
Ink the face of the rubber stamp with the embossing ink and make the impression on the tag.

 STEP 3
Cover the image with gold embossing powder. Remove the excess and return it to the pot.

 STEP 4
Use the heat tool to emboss the design.

 STEP 5
Colour the design with your choice of brush pen colours. I have used yellow, orange and green, and brown for the pot, but the choice is entirely up to you. Leave the centre of the sunflower clear.

 STEP 6
Open the tube of liquid appliqué. It has a small nozzle and you can use it as you would use a pen.
    Make sure that you completely cover the area you wish to be coloured. Do not try to spread the liquid appliqué too

Step 5 Colour the embossed design with brush pens.

Step 6 Paint the sunflower centre with yellow liquid appliqué.

thinly. If there are any small gaps or sparsely covered patches, they will not fill in when you heat the work. The effect you are looking for at this stage is that of a smoothly iced cake. Wipe the nozzle and put the top back on to the tube as soon as you have finished.

 Leave the tag to dry overnight. If you try to hurry this process you will get a very uneven finish, so don't be tempted. Put your work to one side at this stage and leave it alone.

 When the liquid appliqué is completely dry, heat it with your heat tool, taking care not to overheat the gold embossing of the design. If you overheat the embossing, it will lose its shine and even flatten and lose the embossed finish. You can see this as it happens, so take care!

As the liquid appliqué is heated, it bubbles and rises off the surface of the card, producing a textured centre to your sunflower.

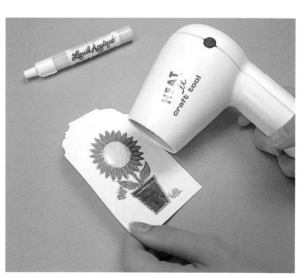

Step 8 After leaving it overnight, heat the liquid appliqué for a raised 3-D effect.

STEP 9 Punch the hole in your tag if you have made your own from card, and thread a piece of ribbon through it to finish off.

Below
Step 9 Punch a hole in the gift tag and thread some ribbon through it.

Below right
The finished gift tag.

For an alternative effect, you can also add a gentle sprinkling of ultra-fine glitter powder to the liquid appliqué when it is still wet. Shower a small amount gently with your fingers, as if you were adding a pinch of salt to some cooking. This will stick to the wet liquid appliqué and when you heat it, the sparkle will still show. This is particularly effective when you are using white liquid appliqué as snow in part of your design.

Gift tag shapes

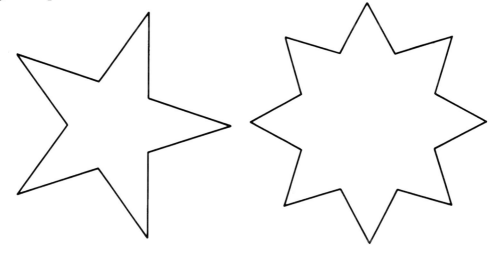

Gift tag shapes

USING
EMBOSSING PENS

Project New baby announcement card

The arrival of a new baby in the family is certainly an event that you want to tell everyone about and it's one of the times when you need to print information that you cannot find on a rubber stamp – the all important details of your baby.

For this project I have used embossing pens. They contain the same kind of special, slow-drying ink that the embossing pads have, and can therefore be coated in gold, silver or coloured embossing powder and heated to give a raised, printed effect to your writing. You can also use them to add lines to a design or to create a border or frame to your work.

The standard embossing pens are available in a variety of nib styles: chisel for italic writing, brush for a more informal style, fine pointed, and there is even a type of ball-point for when you want to add a lot of information. The effect is dependent on the type of pen and I have written the name James in three different pens, embossing in gold powder to demonstrate the different styles (see above).

Embossing pens are also available in a number of colours which you can emboss with the clear powder to enhance the colour of the ink. Many of the pens have dual nibs: a chisel, italic nib at one end and a fine point for more detailed writing at the other.

Embossing pens come in various colours and types of nibs to produce different effects.

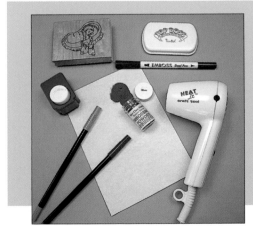

Materials and equipment

Babes & Bunnies (© Inca no. 637-I)
Embossing ink pad
Silver embossing powder
Peach-coloured card
Embossing pen
Brush pens
Corner cutter
Heat tool

Method

 STEP 1 Ink the rubber stamp with an embossing pad and make the impression on the card.

 STEP 2 Cover the print with silver embossing powder, remove the excess and return it to the pot. Heat the image with the heat tool.

STEP 3 Colour the crib image using the brush pens. Subtle colours are more appropriate for a baby card and you can choose pink shades for a girl and blue for a boy if you prefer.

Step 4 Add writing to the design with an embossing pen.

 STEP 4 Design your wording on a separate sheet of paper before you begin to write on the actual card. The ink in the embossing pen dries slowly, so you have plenty of time to finish writing your message before you have to add the powder.

Standard embossing pens use the same type of almost clear ink that you find in an embossing ink pad. This can make it difficult to see what you have written. So that you can see what I have done in the example, I have used a purple embossing pen.

 STEP 5 Once you have finished your message, cover the design with silver embossing powder. Remove the excess. If you have used a standard embossing pen, your words will be known only to you at this stage!

STEP 6 Heat the powder gently to bring out your writing in embossed silver.

Step 6 Heat the powder-covered writing to turn it into silver embossing.

STEP 7

Use the corner punch to round off the corners of the card. You can get corner cutters in a number of different styles such as Nostalgia and Art Deco (both supplied by Fiskars). All of them add a stylish finish to a card, and for this design I have used a curved punch to simply round off the corners of the design.

In order to get an even, smooth curve, it is important to insert the card properly into the corner cutter. Slip the card into the punch, do not force it; it should sit comfortably in the guide space. Make sure that you put it in at an even angle. If you don't, the cut itself will be uneven instead of a smooth curve from one straight edge to the other. Try it out first on a spare piece of card. The difference between the right and wrong technique is very obvious and you will soon get the feel of this very useful tool.

STEP 8

As this design has rabbits in it, I have finished it off by using white liquid appliqué to give them fluffy tails.

The different types of nibs available in the embossing pens give you a wide scope when designing your work. The italic pens can be used for large flowing letters or to add elegant swirls and lines to your design.

If you choose the dual-ended pens, you can use the two different tips to produce different styles of writing on the same design, as I did with the red pen, finishing off the overall design by creating a border in red around the finished card.

The fine-pointed embossing pens are useful if you want to add a great deal of information to a design. You can even write a short letter and emboss your writing, using an embossing powder that will complement the colour of your paper.

Another thing you can do with coloured embossing pens is to actually draw with them or add colour to a design that you have already printed and embossed. For example, you could print and emboss a rose spray in silver, colour it with red and green embossing pens, then add clear or sparkling embossing powder and emboss the colour as well.

The finished card with curved corners and liquid appliqué added to the bunnies' tails.

USING SPECIAL
SCISSORS

Project **Party invitation**

A party invitation is something that should really grab the attention. It has to be noticed, remembered and acted upon! So, if you want more than the standard printed sheets that you can buy in the stationery shop, what better way to get exactly the feel you want for your party than using your own rubber stamp art?

For this project I have taken standard sheets of white card, chosen a cake rubber stamp that gives the right feel for a birthday party, and another rubber stamp for the words of the invitation.

The wording stamp can be teamed up with many other designs to create invitations for different types of birthday party: adult, child, teenage or one of those special milestones such as 30, 40 or 50. You can also create invitations for a dinner party, a Halloween party, New Year celebration, silver wedding party or any other event you would like to celebrate. So a standard invitation wording rubber stamp is a good investment for your collection.

In this project, the extra detail has been added with a pair of decorative craft scissors. Everyone is familiar with the pinking or zig-zag scissors that lurk in the bottom of the sewing basket, but nowadays there is an amazing variety of edged scissors.

Fiskars regularly introduce new designs to their range, which already includes all sorts of different effects such as Zig-Zag, Stamp Perforations, Waves, Victoriana and Ripple.

There are different ways to use the edgers. You can edge a single sheet of card, as I have done in this project, to add interest to a simple piece of work, or, if you want to emphasise the effect, you can add colour to the edge with coloured embossing pens and embossing powder. In later projects I will show you some other ways to add extra interest with the help of a few pairs of edgers.

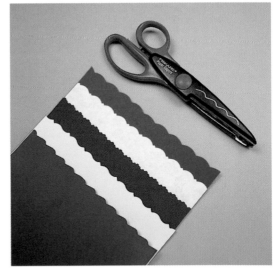

A selection of the finishes that can be achieved with different pairs of edgers. The Wave Edger shown has been used on the dark blue card.

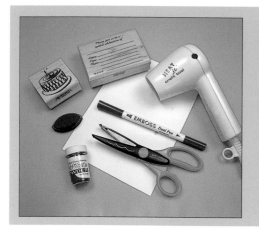

Materials and equipment

Swirl Cake (© All Night Media no. 216F)
Special Celebration (© Mostly Animals no. 765-S8)
Sheet of A5 white card
Red pigment ink pad
Red Sparkle embossing powder
    (supplied by First Class Stamps)
Clouds Paper Edgers (supplied by Fiskars)
Red embossing pen
Heat tool

Method

STEP 1

Ink the Swirl Cake rubber stamp with the red pigment ink pad and make the impression on the card.

Even though I have used a red sparkling embossing powder in this project, which would anyway form a red print on a clear base of embossing ink, I have used a red pigment as the base ink for the design. This will give the final print more depth and any part of the print that is not completely covered with the embossing powder will still show as red in the finished work rather than sparsely covered or blank altogether.

STEP 2

For this design, I wanted to use only part of the party invitation stamp; I wanted the words but not the lines.

To achieve this, you should not ink the rubber stamp face with the embossing pad, but instead use a red embossing pen and colour the face of the rubber as we did for the jam labels in Chapter 3. The ink will stay wet because it dries more slowly than the ink from an ordinary water-based brush pen.

Colour the sections you want and make the second impression on the card.

Step 3 Cover the entire design with the Red Sparkle embossing powder.

STEP 3

Cover the entire design, words and picture, with the Red Sparkle embossing powder. This works in the same way as the other embossing powders that we have used, but this time the glitter or sparkle is combined with the bright red powder. Remove the excess powder and return it to the pot.

STEP 4

Heat the design with the heat tool. As the embossing powder melts you will see that it forms a print with built-in sparkle. This is a permanent part of your print and will not rub or fall off if the powder is properly melted. If it begins to lose its sparkle, it means that you are overheating the print.

STEP 5

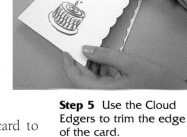

Cut the edge of the card with the Cloud Paper Edgers. Most edgers have a very distinct flow to the pattern and it is worth taking the time to match up this pattern each time you move the blades of the scissors for the next cut.

Each type of edge will give a different effect to your overall design (see page 65). Some are highly decorative, such as Victoriana or Colonial, and will help you to produce quite a formal feel to your work. Others are more informal and produce work with a more casual style. Ripple and Wave are good examples of the latter.

Make sure that you leave enough space on your finished card to write the details of your party!

Step 5 Use the Cloud Edgers to trim the edge of the card.

STEP 6

Carefully draw around the edge of the cut pattern to emphasise the design and give a professional-looking finish to your invitations. You can do this with a plain red pen but I have used the red embossing pen and then embossed it again with the Red Sparkle to give a completed look to the finished invitation (see right).

Different coloured card and embossing powders, as well as different rubber stamps, can help you achieve completely different invitations. Instead of red ink and powder on white card, you could try white glitter embossing powder on red card, or tone the colours by putting purple ink on lilac card. You can also use the edgers in different ways; just shape the corners and emphasise the otherwise straight edges to produce an Art Deco feel.

The finished invitation with the shaped edge highlighted in red.

If you want to use a background colour on which to mount the design, you can give it extra texture, as I have in the Leafy Invitation from Magenta (see page 64). Take a rubber stamp design – in this case I used small, individual leaves – and stamp using an embossing pad and clear embossing powder. Cover the card with the random design. It will create a finish that resembles a textured velvet or rich, textured wallpaper.

COMBINING
TECHNIQUES II

Project **Birthday card**

You have now worked through a number of different techniques to create different types of rubber stamping art. In this project, you will see how many of these techniques can be used together to create something special and unique. This is where you can really begin to use your creativity and skills to the full: making decisions about colour combinations, styles and framing, as well as the rubber stamp design, colour of embossing and colouring of the design.

When you put all of these decisions together to make one design for a card, the possibilities are so endless that the work truly does become an original piece of artwork.

As you are about to create a unique piece of work, first of all take some time to consider the person you are making the card for. One of the real pleasures of rubber stamping is that you can create something personal rather than being limited to the choice of cards available in the shops. No matter how wide the choice is, there is rarely something that is just right!

Look at the papers and card that you have, or that you can find in the craft shops, stationery outlets or your rubber stamp supplier.

You can buy packs of ready-folded blank cards with envelopes. These are available in a variety of colours, plain white, pastels or bright colours, as well as some textured cards or recycled card, but they do limit you to the size of card that is on offer.

If you decide to make your own folded card from a sheet of plain card, your choice is wider. You can easily find packs of A4 sheets of card from stationers, and you can get some wonderful colours, including vivid Day-Glo colours, black, bright red, gold or silver, even hologram.

When you use sheets of card rather than pre-folded card, the first decision you make is the size of your finished card. You also need to consider whether you will be able to find an envelope for it! Once you have made this decision, cut the card to the size you require and use a scoring tool, metal rule and cutting mat to make a folding line. With the right tools and method, you will achieve a neat, professional finish.

Materials and equipment

Wisteria (© Rubber Stampede no. A1666H)
Happy Birthday (© Stamps Unlimited)
Embossing ink pad
Gold embossing powder
Seagull Paper Edgers (supplied by Fiskars)
Piece of white card
Pink paper
White folded card
Brush pens
Glue pen
Heat tool

Method

Ink the Wisteria rubber stamp and make the impression on the separate piece of card. Cover with gold embossing powder, returning the excess powder to the pot.

Step 2 Heat the powder to create the gold embossed image.

Heat the powder to form the embossed image.

Colour the wisteria with the brush pens. I have used the natural colours of green and lilac, but you could choose any combinations you want.

Cut the edge of the card with the Seagull Paper Edgers to create a decorative finish. Take care to keep the flow of the pattern with each new cut.

Step 4 Cut the edge of
the wisteria print with
the Seagull Paper Edgers.

STEP 5 Cut a piece of pink paper slightly larger than your finished wisteria image. Make sure that it will fit comfortably on your folded card, there should be a border left around the coloured layer of your design when the card is constructed.

STEP 6 Glue the wisteria image to the pink paper using a glue pen. Make sure that the wisteria image is properly centred on the pink, creating an even frame.

Step 6 Glue the wisteria
image to the pink
background paper.

STEP 7 Place the combined image on to your folded card to check the placing for the birthday message. You can make a very light pencil mark with a soft lead pencil to indicate the positioning of your final design, but remember that you must be able to erase it cleanly. Set the combined image to one side while you complete the card.

STEP 8 Ink the Happy Birthday rubber stamp and make the impression on the card where it will form part of the completed design. Cover the image with gold embossing powder, returning the excess to the pot.

Step 8 Print Happy Birthday on the creased, blank card.

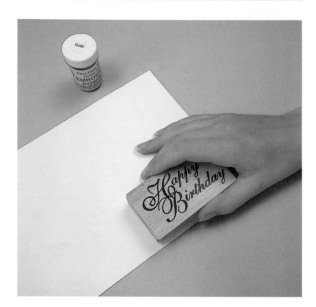

STEP 9

Heat the image to melt the powder.

STEP 10

Glue the framed wisteria image in place on the card, ensuring that it is properly positioned and that you have left enough space above the Happy Birthday message.

There are many different ways of using this combination of techniques. In fact, you are only limited by your imagination and you can use a single rubber stamp design to create very different cards by printing with a variety of colours and a range of background materials.

Almost anything that can be cut and stuck to paper or card can be used as your framing material. Think of the items on this list and see what ideas they inspire:

- Dress fabrics
- Lace trim or scraps of lace curtain
- Unusual wallpaper
- Scraps of wrapping paper
- Sweet wrappers
- Dried leaves or flower petals
- Colourful feathers
- Raffia
- Photocopies of sheet music

The frame doesn't have to completely surround the printed image. It can lie diagonally behind it, you can position the image asymmetrically, or create an irregular or a double frame. Experiment with different textures and different styles until you produce something that is entirely your own.

The finished card with the wisteria print in place.

USING MULBERRY PAPER

Project **Christmas card**

For this project you will be using similar techniques as those for the birthday card, but as Christmas is a very special time of the year, and because Christmas cards have a distinctive look, this time the printing is finished with a sparkling embossing powder and special mulberry paper is used for the frame.

Mulberry paper is very popular in rubber stamp art and it can be used to obtain all sorts of effects. You will probably have to get it from your rubber stamp supplier, or you may be able to find it in a specialist craft shop.

Mulberry paper is a soft-textured paper, with irregular colouring and pieces of fibre and bark forming part of the finish. It can be cut with scissors to give a straight edge, and you will still be able to see the texture of the paper, but it really comes into its own when you tear the paper carefully. This produces a unique feathered effect as parts of the fibre pull away from the edges of the paper.

The colour range is quite good, from white and pale pastels such as pink and lilac, to deep colours, such as forest green, scarlet and purple which are perfect for Christmas cards. Some of the colours are also available with small strips of gold tinsel incorporated into the paper.

Although I have used it as a framing paper for the printed images in this project, you can also print and emboss directly on to the mulberry paper itself. You must remember however, that mulberry paper is lighter than standard paper, so take care not to scorch it when heating the embossing powder.

Materials and equipment

Ribbon Angel (© All Night Media no. 240J)
Peace on Earth (© Mostly Animals no. 354–S4)
Small piece of white card
White folded card
Purple mulberry paper
Clear, sparkling embossing powder
Black embossing ink pad
Brush pens
Heat tool
Ripple Paper Edgers (supplied by Fiskars)
Glue pen

Method

STEP 1

Sparkling embossing powders can have a base of either clear or coloured powder. As this one is clear, the colour of the embossing ink will form part of your design. I have chosen black ink as this will produce a sparkling black outline to the angel.

Ink the Ribbon Angel rubber stamp with black embossing ink and make the impression on the piece of card. Cover the impression with sparkling embossing powder, remove the excess and return it to the pot.

STEP 2

Heat the embossing powder. You have to take extra care when you heat sparkling embossing powders, because too much heat can burn the sparkling flecks in the powder. Work in good light, preferably daylight, and watch your work carefully as you add the heat. You can see the powder change from a dull powder to a glossy finish (as in all embossing), and from the glittering image that you want to a duller, flatter finish if you overheat it. You will soon learn to recognise the different stages!

STEP 3

Colour your image using the coloured brush pens. I have chosen pale, delicate shades for the Christmas angel, but you may prefer a more vivid palette.

STEP 4

Cut the edge of your coloured image with the Ripple Paper Edgers. Measure the cut card against your folded card to check that you have allowed enough space for the mulberry paper frame.

Step 4 Cut out the angel image with Ripple Paper Edgers.

Step 5 Tear the mulberry paper carefully, pulling it apart approximately 1in (2–3cm) at a time to achieve a feathered effect.

STEP 5

Open out the sheet of mulberry paper and lay it on a flat surface. Although you can tear a square large enough to fit behind your angel image and simply stick the two together, this is a wasteful way of using the mulberry paper. It is more economical to tear four strips and use them to frame the angel image. The fact that it is an unevenly textured paper means that you can piece together the strips easily without the joins being obvious.

Tear the paper slowly and gently. It will take a little while to get used to this. Tear along one edge, pulling the paper away gently with one hand while you hold it firmly with the other. Keep your hands very close together and only tear about 1in (2–3cm) at a time to keep the tear fairly even and to make the most of the feathered effect of the paper.

You can use a paintbrush to paint a wet line down the mulberry paper. This will help you to pull the fibres apart more easily, but you then have to wait for it to dry and I find that the feathered edge is not as pronounced when you use this technique.

Step 6 Glue the strips of mulberry paper to the back of the angel image.

Once you have the strips of paper that you want, run a strip of craft glue, such as PVA, or a glue pen, along one side of the back of your angel image and stick the mulberry paper to it. Concentrate on the effect from the front; don't worry about how even it is at the back.

If you are using a new sheet of mulberry paper or have previously cut a piece from the sheet, one side of your strip may be more textured than the other, use that as the outer edge that will show in your final design. If you have any gaps in your frame, simply tear off a small extra piece of paper and fill in the gap.

Although you can piece the mulberry paper together without it being noticeable, try not to overlap the strips or pieces. The double layer will look darker or more dense than the rest of your design.

Once the mulberry frame is in place and the glue has dried, position the combined image on your card to check the spacing for your Christmas message. You can use a soft lead pencil to make a light mark at this stage, but do remember that you will want to remove this from your completed card.

Ink the Peace on Earth rubber stamp with black embossing ink and make the impression on your folded card. Cover with sparkling embossing powder and return any excess to the pot. Heat the image carefully to melt the powder.

Using a glue that will not distort the card, stick the framed angel image on to your folded card.

Mulberry paper can be used on all sorts of different designs to add interest and texture to your rubber stamp art. Use it as we have in this project, to create a frame for a rubber stamp design, or use it in small feathered squares and rectangles to create a collage effect. You can also use it as wrapping paper for special gifts, or to cover gift boxes.

Mulberry paper is very thin and fibrous, so you must take extra care if you actually print on to it. Do not use too much ink, as it could bleed and spoil the image. Working on top of a bed of paper towels will help to absorb any excess ink. If you are printing on to mulberry paper, remember to make the most of the texture of the fibres in the paper rather than swamping them with the design.

The completed Christmas card.

COMBINING
EMBOSSING
POWDERS

Project **Gift bag**

For most of your rubber stamp art you will decide on and use a single colour of embossing powder: gold flowers, silver angels, red hearts or clear powder over rainbow-coloured inks. But it is possible to achieve a multicoloured effect with different powders rather than clear powder over different coloured inks. It is certainly a more difficult technique, it takes more time and patience, but the effect can be wonderful. The colours seem to glow as the light hits your work at different angles.

This is a technique that works really well with gold, silver, copper and bronze powders, because the metallic nature of these powders results in a subtle glow when they are treated in this way. You can also use bright or primary-coloured powders, as I did with the stencil fish, but this can be very similar to the effect of clear powder over coloured inks and you will have to decide which method you would prefer to use for a bright finish.

To make the most of the work, it is best to use three colours and to choose a rubber stamp design that will show off the work you have put into your printing.

There are two ways of using the different powders. For the first method, which I have used in this project and in the tiger-print bag, individual prints are embossed using different metallic powders. This takes time, because you have to work with separate areas or lines of your design, inking, making the impression, adding powder and embossing as you go, but it is the easier method.

In the second method, which you can move on to when you feel more confident, you add the different powders to sections of the same impression. Falling leaves are a perfect choice for this type of work. The rubber stamp design is large enough to take the different colours, and the design itself suits the shading effect.

You work with a single impression on the paper at a time. Use a spoon to add some gold embossing powder to the top of the print first, remove the excess carefully, ensuring that it does not fall across the rest of the wet ink. Then add the silver to the middle section, again using a spoon to place it exactly where you want it. Once more, take care that it does not fall across the third, unpowdered part of the print, but you don't have to worry about the gold section; once that is powdered a second colour will not adhere to the ink. Finally, add the copper to the rest of the leaf image, remove the excess, add the heat to melt the powders and move on to repeat the process with a second print.

You can buy plain gift bags to decorate, but for this project I have started with a roll of strong craft paper, available from most stationery outlets. You can use almost any type of paper, as long as it will be strong enough to hold a gift when it is finished. Brown paper or craft paper is ideal, but you could use a plain wallpaper, lining paper or even a very lightweight card.

Materials and equipment

Supercube (© Superstamp no. K6503)
Roll of craft paper
Embossing ink pad
Gold, silver and copper embossing powders
Pencil or pen
Cutting mat and craft knife
Metal rule
Glue
Heat tool
Hole punch
Ribbon or cord for handles

Method

STEP 1

Draw or trace the template for the bag on to your paper. The size can be increased or decreased to make different-sized gift bags. To make a bag the size of the one shown in the photographs, you will need to enlarge the template by 141% (on a photocopier, this means an enlargement from A4 to A3). The main thing to remember is that if you make a large bag the paper must be strong enough to hold the gift safely. A more detailed explanation of how to make a gift bag can be found at the end of this project.

STEP 2

Place the paper on the cutting mat and use a craft knife to cut out the bag. Make sure that you do not cut any of the fold lines.

It is important to decide on your final design for the bag before you start printing. At this stage, the paper is still flat, with the fold lines marked but not formed. This makes it easier to do your rubber stamping, but you do have to remember that although it is a sheet of two-dimensional paper at this stage, it will eventually be a three-dimensional gift bag.

Ink the face of the rubber stamp that you have decided to use. The Supercube has several faces, so you could use a different face for each colour.

Stamp a diagonal line of impressions across the section of the bag that will eventually form the front. Re-ink the stamp before each impression to ensure that you get a similar amount of embossing powder on each print.

Step 4 Begin the first line of printing.

Cover the line of rubber stamp impressions with silver embossing powder, remove the excess and return it to the pot.

Use the heat tool to emboss this first line of the design.

Print a second line of images to one side of the first. Cover them with copper embossing powder, remove the excess and return it to the pot.

Heat this line of images, taking care not to overheat those images which are already embossed. It is very important to remember that overheating can scorch the finished embossing and make it dull and flat.

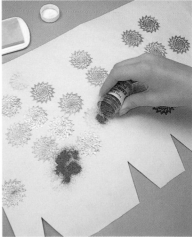

Repeat the process with each line of prints until you have filled the paper. You can either print very closely – as with the tiger print (see page 80) – which will emphasise the different colours of the embossing, or you can leave more empty space in your design, as I have in this project. This allows the colour of your paper to show through.

Step 9 Add more lines of printing and emboss using different coloured embossing powders.

STEP 10

Once the printing is finished and cooled, score along the fold lines, fold them and glue the bag together. If you want your gift bag to carry a heavy or fragile gift, glue a thick piece of card into the base.

The finished bag printed in gold, silver and copper.

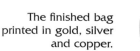

STEP 11

Use the hole punch to put holes in the top of the bag and thread ribbon or cord through them to form handles.

The technique of using different coloured embossing powders can take a little time to master and if you are using different colours on a single print, you must make sure that you have chosen a rubber stamp design that is large enough to take them; it is impossible to be absolutely accurate with the placing of the powders.

It is worth practising this method on some spare paper until you feel comfortable working with it before moving on to your actual piece of artwork. Once you have mastered it, you will find that you can make your printing look really special.

Making a gift bag

1. Draw or trace the bag template on to strong paper. You can use a photocopier to make it larger or smaller.
2. Cut along the solid lines.

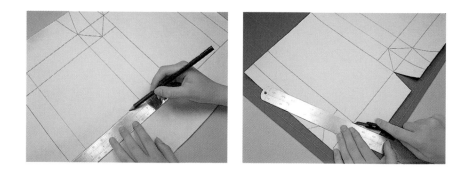

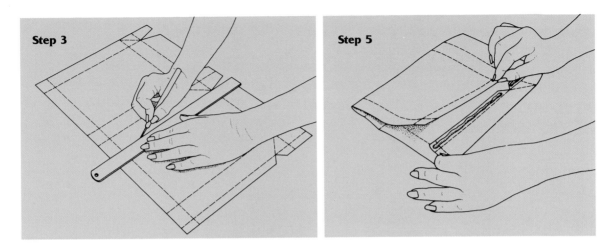

3. Score along the dotted lines with a scoring tool and a metal rule. Or, transpose steps 2 and 3: score along the fold lines before cutting out.

4. When you have completed your rubber stamping, pre-crease all of the folds, then fold along all the vertical lines to create the shape of the bag.

5. Glue strip A–A to B–B, making sure that you keep the lines of the bag straight, otherwise you will make a crooked bag!

6. Fold inwards the strip along the top of the bag.

7. Lay the bag flat on the table so that crease C–C is uppermost. (As you flatten the bag, make sure that the vertical side creases (D–D) turn inwards.) Then turn the base up at crease C–C. All the parts which make up the base should now be splayed out, flat, and facing up towards you.

8. Fold in the sides of the base and put a blob of glue on to each one.

The bag shown in these drawings is larger than that shown in the photographs on page 84. This is so that you can see clearly what is being done at each step.

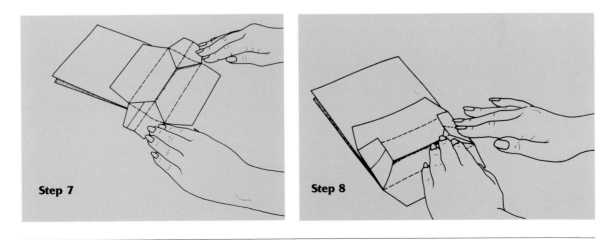

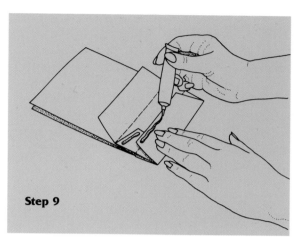

Step 9

9. Fold in the two longer strips which form the rest of the base and press them down on to the glue. These two strips overlap slightly, so you may wish to put some glue under the overlap to make sure that the base is completely stuck down and secure. You can now unfold the base, expand the bag and stand it upright.

10. Use a hole punch to put holes in the top of the bag and thread some cord for the handles through them.

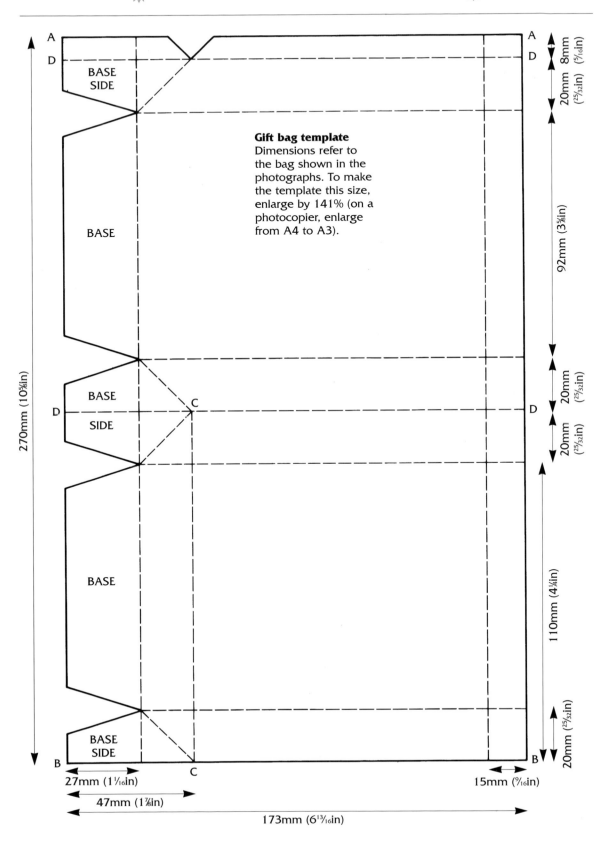

Gift bag template
Dimensions refer to the bag shown in the photographs. To make the template this size, enlarge by 141% (on a photocopier, enlarge from A4 to A3).

BASE SIDE

BASE

BASE SIDE

BASE

BASE SIDE

8mm (⁵/₁₆in)

20mm (²⁵/₃₂in)

92mm (3⅝in)

20mm (²⁵/₃₂in)

20mm (²⁵/₃₂in)

110mm (4¼in)

20mm (²⁵/₃₂in)

270mm (10⅝in)

27mm (1¹/₁₆in)

47mm (1⅞in)

15mm (⁹/₁₆in)

173mm (6¹³/₁₆in)

WORKING WITH
LARGE AREAS

Project **Special event notice**

Rubber stamp art does not have to be restricted to small items. In fact, it can really make a difference to a larger piece of work, turning a plain notice into a full-colour piece of artwork. The fact that each notice has been individually printed and coloured will make it look even more impressive.

Posters for concerts, charity sales, fund raisers or any other type of event can be made much more eye-catching with the right choice of rubber stamp art.

Materials and equipment

Bride and Groom (© Personal Impressions no. 255R)
Champagne Glass (© Personal Impressions no. 148N)
Wedding Bells (© Personal Impressions no. 64D)
Card or paper
Embossing ink pad
Silver embossing powder
Brush pens
Heat tool

STEP 1

Once you have decided what you would like to say on the poster and what overall style you want to use, it is important to plan the layout. Take into account both the words and the rubber stamp art you will be using, as they have to work together.

Method

Make a sketch of your design first, just working out roughly the positions of the words and pictures. You will probably try a few different designs before you begin to finalise a definite look. Don't forget, you can use your paper in landscape format (wider than it is tall) as well as the more obvious portrait format (taller than it is wide).

Step 1 Draw a rough layout of the poster design.

A particular problem to avoid is that of placing the words beautifully and then having to squash your pictures into a corner. If you have planned the layout properly, the poster will look very empty before you add your rubber stamping.

 Once you are happy with your plan, prepare the wording of the poster in whichever way you have chosen – on a computer, with calligraphy or with stencils. If you are going to produce a number of copies on a printer or photocopier, this is the stage to do it, because the rubber stamp art must be original to each poster; photocopying the designs would be breaking the copyright restrictions.

 Ink the Wedding Bells rubber stamp and make the impression on the poster. Always work from the top of the poster downwards when adding a number of impressions. This will prevent you from smudging your work.

Cover the design with silver embossing powder, removing the excess and returning it to the pot. Emboss the image with your heat tool.

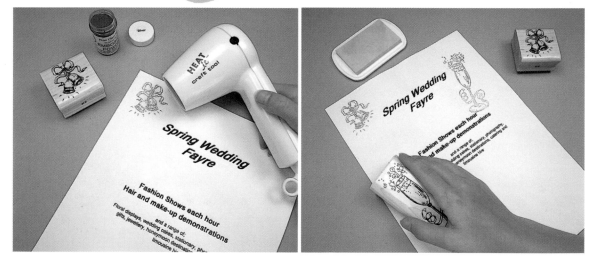

Step 4 Emboss the first rubber stamp print on the poster.

Step 5 Add further designs to the poster and emboss them.

STEP 5

Continue to add the different designs as you work down the poster. If you work quickly enough and take care not to smudge one impression while you make another, you can make a number of prints on the poster before adding the embossing powder, or you can decide to leave the heating stage until you have printed and added embossing powder to a number of prints.

As you do more and more rubber stamping, you will learn how long you can leave each stage and how quickly you are able to work, but if you decide to use these techniques, do remember that the powder is loose until it is heated, and if you leave it too long the underlying ink will dry and the powder will simply fall off.

STEP 6

Once you have finished printing and embossing, add colour to your design to make the poster really eye-catching.

Colouring each individual poster is very effective, but the more designs you use and the more intricate the designs, the

The finished poster with colour added to the embossed prints.

longer they will take to colour. This is fine if you have a very small number of posters to complete, or if you want to make the preparations for the event a team project with a number of people working together.

If, on the other hand, you have to produce a large number of posters more quickly, use the rainbow ink pad technique that was used for the writing paper in Chapter 7. For this method to work effectively, you should use rubber stamp designs that have a lot of detail. This will help to give you a lot of ink, and therefore colour, on your poster design.

You can create many different styles of work by choosing your rubber stamp designs carefully. I have used some very intricate designs from Magenta to produce a formal, almost Victorian style, for the flower show poster (see page 88), while the teddy bears' picnic poster has been given a feeling of fun with a range of classic teddy bear rubber stamps from Stamps Unlimited.

USING A
REPEATED DESIGN

Project **Photo frame**

Photographs, especially family photographs, are treasured objects and rather than lying untended in a drawer or forgotten in a photo album, they deserve pride of place in your home.

Making your own picture frames is a wonderful way to create a beautiful display of photographs for your wall or table top. The fact that you make each one yourself means that you have complete control over the size, style, colour and image of your collection.

You can buy rubber stamps that print as a complete frame and these are ideal for small photographs. You can use these designs to produce an aperture card or a small frame for a special photograph: a baby's christening, a child's first day in school uniform, a graduation picture, a family photo for Christmas or a wedding photograph. The finished frame makes the photograph look that much more special and it's an ideal way to turn a simple snapshot into a great gift.

Although the frame design rubber stamps are very useful stamps to add to your collection, in this project we will be dealing with larger frames and the design will be made up of a smaller image repeated and combined in new ways. This will introduce the technique of masking to your repertoire of rubber stamping skills.

Masking is a method of using a simple rubber stamp design to create a far more complex, multiple image. It is more than just the simple repeat printing that we used in earlier projects such as the wrapping paper and bookmark. Masking creates a new design by using a combination of impressions.

In most examples of masking, the full impression of the stamp is only seen once; it will be the first impression you make. From that point onwards, only a part of the design is printed as you cover the base paper or card. The result is a complete, single design covering your entire work surface, without any interruption to the flow.

The most important part of the masking technique is actually cutting an accurate mask. You must be able to cut very closely and exactly around the rubber stamp design. It is best, therefore, to choose a fairly simple rubber stamp as your basic design. Once you feel more confident with the technique you can move on to more complex outlines such as the bunch of balloons that I have used for the baby frame (see page 92).

Materials and equipment

Autumn Leaves (© Rubber Stampede no. A1607H)
Embossing ink pad
Copper embossing powder
Sheet of mounting board
Sheet of acetate
Blue card
Black embossing ink pad
Clear embossing powder
Cutting mat
Metal rule
Craft knife
Heat tool
Masking tape
Glue

Method

STEP 1

Once you have decided on your rubber stamp design and the photograph you wish to frame, you will be able to make some decisions as to the actual size of the frame you will be making.

The interior aperture of your frame will be governed by the amount of the photograph you want to see. This is an ideal way to crop a photograph and get rid of unwanted background detail, or to change a full-length photograph into a head and shoulders portrait. You do not have to restrict yourself to a square or oblong aperture, you can cut an oval, a circle or even a diamond or heart if you want to.

The width of the frame that will surround the aperture is dependent on the rubber stamp design you have picked. The space will have to be wide enough to take the design but not so wide that the image will look lost. Make a paper template of your frame at this stage to check that you have allowed enough space for the rubber stamping design and your photograph.

STEP 2 When you have finalised your frame design, draw the exterior measurements on to the sheet of mounting board. You will need to cut two pieces of board, one for the front and a second for the back.

Set aside one piece. Take the second and mark out the aperture. Cut this out carefully with the craft knife, taking care not to cut beyond the corners you have marked, because this is the front of your frame and any errors will show.

STEP 3 Turn your frame over and print on the other, unmarked side. Ink your rubber stamp with embossing ink and make the first impression. It is normally best to start at a corner of the frame rather than in the centre, because this is the widest section and will give you most scope for printing the full design.

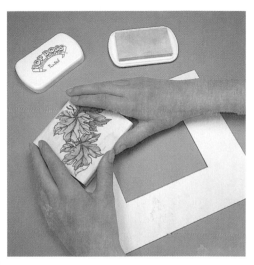

Step 3 Make the first impression in the corner of the frame.

STEP 4 Cover the impression with the copper embossing powder and remove the excess. When you are working with multiple images, it is important to take care when handling the card. Try to keep it clear of finger prints or other grease marks; the embossing powder will stick to these marks as you build up the design and will be difficult to brush off. Eventually it will spoil the work altogether.

STEP 5 Take a spare piece of card to make your mask. Coloured card is the easiest to use, because you can see it clearly against your background. Having cleaned your rubber stamp, ink it with the black embossing ink and make the impression. Then, cover it with clear embossing powder, remove the excess and emboss with the heat tool.

STEP 6 Embossing the image for your mask will make it easier to cut around accurately, because you can be guided by the raised edge. Take great care with this stage; do not be tempted to cut roughly around the design. This mask must cover the first impression you made exactly, allowing you to make a second impression, partly over the mask and partly on to the frame.

Step 6 Print a mask on different coloured card and cut it out carefully.

Clean the rubber stamp thoroughly to remove all traces of black pigment ink before continuing with your frame.

STEP 7 Place the mask over the first impression, lining it up exactly so that it completely covers the design. The aim is to create a second impression that looks as if it is half hidden by the first.

If you use an informal design such as the falling leaves I have chosen here, you should be able to study the finished work and not be entirely sure where one design ends and the other begins.

Ink the rubber stamp and make the impression carefully. Part of your new print will be on the mask.

Cover the image in embossing powder. Remove the excess and heat the powder with the heat tool. You must emboss each individual image as you go, otherwise you will smudge the underlying image when you place the mask over it.

Step 8 Use the mask to build up the design of the frame.

STEP 8 Repeat the process, covering your second impression with the mask and printing over it. In this case I have covered the first impression again and made the third on the other side of it.

You should alter the amount of the design that is printed on the mask each time, to give a flow to your finished design. Sometimes you can just print the very edge of the design on the mask, leaving most of the design showing on your frame, at other times you can have far more of the design hidden behind the previous impression.

With the falling leaves design, I have also turned the rubber stamp around. The first impression is in the corner, with the stalks of the leaves pointing to the right. As I printed along the bottom of the frame, the stalks pointed towards the first set. On the other parts of the frame I printed the leaves so that their tips were touching. This informal method of printing gives you an overall design that resembles the jumbled look of a woodland floor in autumn.

STEP 9

Continue building up your design in this manner until you have filled your frame. If you are left with any blank spaces along the edges of your frame, you can add a very small amount of the design, such as the tip of a leaf.

STEP 10

Cut a piece of acetate just smaller than your frame size. You can buy sheets of acetate in an art shop, or you can use a sheet of overhead projector film, available in any office stationery shop.

Tape the acetate to the back of the printed frame, covering the aperture. Fix in place with masking tape.

STEP 11

Place your photograph behind the acetate. Make sure that you place it straight on its new frame, otherwise it will annoy you forever. Once you are happy with the way it is placed in the frame, tape along the top of the photograph with masking tape.

STEP 12

Glue the second piece of mounting card in place to form the back of the frame. Fasten a mounting hook, a piece of string or a stand on the back. Stand back and admire your work.

The design will begin to flow seamlessly as you work.

If you would prefer to be able to change the photographs in your frame, you can glue the back in place after fixing the acetate, leaving one edge of the frame unglued. You can then slip another photograph into place at any time.

The masking technique suits a rubber stamp design that has very definite and solid edges to it, such as the autumn leaves (see page 92). This makes it easier to cut and place the mask accurately, which is very important for an effective finish.

However, once you have mastered the technique, you can experiment with other types of design. The bunch of balloons rubber stamp that I have used for the baby frame (see page 92) is much more detailed. It also has a specific direction in the design – the balloons float up – and it is important to remember this when placing your prints. You don't want to end up with balloons that float upside down.

It isn't always necessary to cover the entire frame with images. Some designs can look very elegant when they are draped across the corners of the frame, leaving the rest plain. If you are planning a design like this, take the colour of your mounting board into account as it will form a much larger part of the overall design.

You can also frame your rubber stamp art, as I have with the lion print from Magenta (see page 92). The detail on this print is so fine that it would be a mistake to swamp it with a heavily decorated frame, so I have used the tiger print rubber stamp design from Rubber Stampede and printed it on a black mounting board frame, using an embossing ink pad and clear embossing powder to create a texture for the frame rather than a pattern.

The finished frame with the photograph inserted.

LIST OF SUPPLIERS

Magenta
351 Blain Mont Saint-Hilare
QC J3H 3B4
Canada
Tel: 001 514 446-5253

Superstamp
Superstamp House
Station Road
Backworth
Tyne & Wear
NE27 0RU
England
Tel: 0191 268 7309

Inca Stamps
136 Stanley Green Road
Poole
BH15 3AH
England
Tel: 01202 777222

Funstamps
144 Neilston Road
Paisley
PA2 6QJ
Scotland
Tel: 0141 884 5007/6441

Stamps Unlimited
16 The Frances
Thatcham
Berkshire
RG18 4LT
England
Tel: 01635 868990

Rubber Stampede
Unit 9 Ashburton Industrial Estate
Ross-On-Wye
Herefordshire
HR9 7BW
England
Tel: 01989 768988

Personal Impressions
and **Mostly Animals**
Curzon Road
Chilton Industrial Estate
Sudbury
Suffolk
CO10 6XW
England
Tel: 01787 375241

(The **Mostly Animals** range is
available in Britain through
Personal Impressions.)

First Class Stamps
and **All Night Media**
Hall Staithe
Fakenham
Norfolk
NR21 9BW
England
Tel: 01328 851449

(The **All Night Media** range is
available through **First Class
Stamps**.)

Fiskars (UK) Ltd
Bridgend Business Centre
Bridgend
Mid-Glamorgan
CF31 3XJ
Tel: 01656 655595

These ranges are also available
through most good rubber stamp
suppliers.

ABOUT
THE AUTHOR

Brenda Hunt has always loved creating things and has been involved in interior and graphic design for almost 20 years, spending 10 of these gathering inspiration as she travelled around the world. She discovered the craft of rubber stamping almost 14 years ago during a visit to America, and was instantly captivated by the quality of the designs that were available. She has been collecting and working with rubber stamps ever since.

She now works from her studio in the north-east of England, using a variety of techniques including rubber stamping to produce a range of hand-printed stationery which she sells by special order and at craft fairs.

INDEX

TITLES AVAILABLE FROM GMC PUBLICATIONS
BOOKS

Woodworking

40 More Woodworking Plans & Projects	GMC Publications
Bird Boxes and Feeders for the Garden	Dave Mackenzie
Complete Woodfinishing	Ian Hosker
Electric Woodwork	Jeremy Broun
Furniture & Cabinetmaking Projects	GMC Publications
Furniture Projects	Rod Wales
Furniture Restoration (Practical Crafts)	Kevin Jan Bonner
Furniture Restoration and Repair for Beginners	Kevin Jan Bonner
Green Woodwork	Mike Abbott
The Incredible Router	Jeremy Broun
Making & Modifying Woodworking Tools	Jim Kingshott
Making Chairs and Tables	GMC Publications
Making Fine Furniture	Tom Darby
Making Little Boxes from Wood	John Bennett
Making Shaker Furniture	Barry Jackson
Pine Furniture Projects for the Home	Dave Mackenzie
Sharpening Pocket Reference Book	Jim Kingshott
Sharpening: The Complete Guide	Jim Kingshott
Stickmaking: A Complete Course	Andrew Jones & Clive George
Woodfinishing Handbook (Practical Crafts)	Ian Hosker
Woodworking Plans and Projects	GMC Publications
The Workshop	Jim Kingshott

Woodturning

Adventures in Woodturning	David Springett
Bert Marsh: Woodturner	Bert Marsh
Bill Jones' Notes from the Turning Shop	Bill Jones
Bill Jones' Further Notes from the Turning Shop	Bill Jones
Colouring Techniques for Woodturners	Jan Sanders
The Craftsman Woodturner	Peter Child
Decorative Techniques for Woodturners	Hilary Bowen
Essential Tips for Woodturners	GMC Publications
Faceplate Turning	GMC Publications
Fun at the Lathe	R.C. Bell
Illustrated Woodturning Techniques	John Hunnex
Intermediate Woodturning Projects	GMC Publications
Keith Rowley's Woodturning Projects	Keith Rowley
Make Money from Woodturning	Ann & Bob Phillips
Multi-Centre Woodturning	Ray Hopper
Pleasure and Profit from Woodturning	Reg Sherwin
Practical Tips for Turners & Carvers	GMC Publications

Practical Tips for Woodturners	GMC Publications
Spindle Turning	GMC Publications
Turning Miniatures in Wood	John Sainsbury
Turning Wooden Toys	Terry Lawrence
Understanding Woodturning	Ann & Bob Phillips
Useful Techniques for Woodturners	GMC Publications
Useful Woodturning Projects	GMC Publications
Woodturning: A Foundation Course	Keith Rowley
Woodturning: A Source Book of Shapes	John Hunnex
Woodturning Jewellery	Hilary Bowen
Woodturning Masterclass	Tony Boase
Woodturning Techniques	GMC Publications
Woodturning Tools & Equipment Test Reports	GMC Publications
Woodturning Wizardry	David Springett

Woodcarving

The Art of the Woodcarver	GMC Publications
Carving Birds & Beasts	GMC Publications
Carving on Turning	Chris Pye
Carving Realistic Birds	David Tippey
Decorative Woodcarving	Jeremy Williams
Essential Tips for Woodcarvers	GMC Publications
Essential Woodcarving Techniques	Dick Onians
Lettercarving in Wood: A Practical Course	Chris Pye
Practical Tips for Turners & Carvers	GMC Publications
Understanding Woodcarving	GMC Publications
Understanding Woodcarving in the Round	GMC Publications
Useful Techniques for Woodcarvers	GMC Publications
Wildfowl Carving - Volume 1	Jim Pearce
Wildfowl Carving - Volume 2	Jim Pearce
The Woodcarvers	GMC Publications
Woodcarving: A Complete Course	Ron Butterfield
Woodcarving: A Foundation Course	Zoë Gertner
Woodcarving for Beginners	GMC Publications
Woodcarving Tools & Equipment Test Reports	GMC Publications
Woodcarving Tools, Materials & Equipment	Chris Pye

Upholstery

Seat Weaving (Practical Crafts)	Ricky Holdstock
Upholsterer's Pocket Reference Book	David James
Upholstery: A Complete Course	David James
Upholstery Restoration	David James
Upholstery Techniques & Projects	David James

TITLES AVAILABLE FROM GMC PUBLICATIONS

Toymaking

Designing & Making Wooden Toys	*Terry Kelly*
Fun to Make Wooden Toys & Games	*Jeff & Jennie Loader*
Making Board, Peg & Dice Games	*Jeff & Jennie Loader*
Making Wooden Toys & Games	*Jeff & Jennie Loader*
Restoring Rocking Horses	*Clive Green & Anthony Dew*
Wooden Toy Projects	*GMC Publications*

Dolls' Houses and Miniatures

Architecture for Dolls' Houses	*Joyce Percival*
Beginners' Guide to the Dolls' House Hobby	*Jean Nisbett*
The Complete Dolls' House Book	*Jean Nisbett*
Dolls' House Bathrooms: Lots of Little Loos	*Patricia King*
Easy to Make Dolls' House Accessories	*Andrea Barham*
Make Your Own Dolls' House Furniture	*Maurice Harper*
Making Dolls' House Furniture	*Patricia King*
Making Georgian Dolls' Houses	*Derek Rowbottom*
Making Miniature Oriental Rugs & Carpets	*Meik & Ian McNaughton*
Making Period Dolls' House Accessories	*Andrea Barham*
Making Period Dolls' House Furniture	*Derek & Sheila Rowbottom*
Making Tudor Dolls' Houses	*Derek Rowbottom*
Making Unusual Miniatures	*Graham Spalding*
Making Victorian Dolls' House Furniture	*Patricia King*
Miniature Bobbin Lace	*Roz Snowden*
Miniature Needlepoint Carpets	*Janet Granger*
The Secrets of the Dolls' House Makers	*Jean Nisbett*

Crafts

A Beginners' Guide to Rubber Stamping	*Brenda Hunt*
Celtic Knotwork Designs	*Sheila Sturrock*
Collage from Seeds, Leaves and Flowers	*Joan Carver*
Complete Pyrography	*Stephen Poole*
Creating Knitwear Designs	*Pat Ashforth & Steve Plummer*
Creative Embroidery Techniques	
Using Colour Through Gold	*Daphne J. Ashby & Jackie Woolsey*
Cross Stitch Kitchen Projects	*Janet Granger*
Cross Stitch on Colour	*Sheena Rogers*
Embroidery Tips & Hints	*Harold Hayes*
An Introduction to Crewel Embroidery	*Mave Glenny*

Making Character Bears	*Valerie Tyler*
Making Greetings Cards for Beginners	*Pat Sutherland*
Making Knitwear Fit	*Pat Ashforth & Steve Plummer*
Needlepoint: A Foundation Course	*Sandra Hardy*
Pyrography Handbook (Practical Crafts)	*Stephen Poole*
Tassel Making for Beginners	*Enid Taylor*
Tatting Collage	*Lindsay Rogers*
Temari: A Traditional Japanese Embroidery Technique	*Margaret Ludlow*

The Home

Home Ownership: Buying and Maintaining	*Nicholas Snelling*
Security for the Householder: Fitting Locks and Other Devices	*E. Phillips*

Videos

Drop-in and Pinstuffed Seats	*David James*
Stuffover Upholstery	*David James*
Elliptical Turning	*David Springett*
Woodturning Wizardry	*David Springett*
Turning Between Centres: The Basics	*Dennis White*
Turning Bowls	*Dennis White*
Boxes, Goblets and Screw Threads	*Dennis White*
Novelties and Projects	*Dennis White*
Classic Profiles	*Dennis White*
Twists and Advanced Turning	*Dennis White*
Sharpening the Professional Way	*Jim Kingshott*
Sharpening Turning & Carving Tools	*Jim Kingshott*
Bowl Turning	*John Jordan*
Hollow Turning	*John Jordan*
Woodturning: A Foundation Course	*Keith Rowley*
Carving a Figure: The Female Form	*Ray Gonzalez*
The Router: A Beginner's Guide	*Alan Goodsell*
The Scroll Saw: A Beginner's Guide	*John Burke*

Magazines

Woodturning • Woodcarving • The Router

Furniture & Cabinetmaking • The Dolls' House Magazine

Creative Crafts For The Home • BusinessMatters

The above represents a full list of all titles currently published or scheduled to be published. All are available direct from the Publishers or through bookshops, newsagents and specialist retailers. To place an order, or to obtain a complete catalogue, contact:

GMC Publications, Castle Place, 166 High Street, Lewes, East Sussex BN7 1XU, United Kingdom
Tel: 01273 488005 Fax: 01273 478606

Orders by credit card are accepted